in the high country!

CONTENTS

ABSOLUTELY
AWESOME 2

MICHAEL & CAROLINE CARROLL

TYNDALE KiDS

TYNDALE HOUSE PUBLISHERS, INC.
WHEATON, ILLINOIS

Visit Tyndale's exciting Web site at www.tyndale.com

Edited by Betty Free

Designed by Jackie Noe

Published in association with the literary agency of Alive Communications, Inc., 7680 Goddard Street, Suite 200, Colorado Springs, CO 80920.

Library of Congress Cataloging-in-Publication data

ISBN 0-8423-5238-4

Printed in Hong Kong

08 07 06 05 04 03 02 01
7   6   5   4   3   2   1

ACKNOWLEDGMENTS

The authors wish to express their appreciation to the following science reviewers. While not actually endorsing the book, they have all read the chapters related to their area of expertise. They have even admitted that each of their areas was accurately represented. (Any mistakes are ours, not theirs.) We thank them for their time and talent. They are, in order of their chapters:

Alyce Todd, Educator, Colorado's Ocean Journey

Scott Elias, fellow of the Institute for Arctic and Alpine Research

Robert Naeye, editor of Mercury magazine, Astronomical Society of the Pacific

Our thanks also go to the tireless work of Jackie Noe, who made us look good visually; Betty Free, who made us sound good verbally; and Karen Watson, whose guiding presence brings joy to any project!

INTRODUCTION

Did you know that

—there are creatures with blue blood?

—some insects have a thousand eyes?

—there are bizarre plants that grow twelve inches a day and others that have exploding fruit?

—there are creatures that live in the dead skeletons of coral reefs?

—a moon of Jupiter has as much power as a million television sets?

—in one place in space the light of a thousand galaxies is bent like a bowl?

—a mighty redwood tree can collapse because of tiny beetles?

—a clown fish can live comfortably within the arms of a deadly sea anemone?

What an absolutely awesome universe!

The Bible contains some of the earliest writings that give us details about our amazing universe. In the book of Isaiah, written 700 years before Christ, we find this statement: "It is God who sits above the circle of the earth" (Isaiah 40:22). In other words, God was telling the ancient world that the earth was round back when everyone thought it was flat. (Well, it *looks* flat, so don't blame them!)

And how about this one: The Bible observes that every star is different. (No, they aren't just lights in the sky, guys.) First Corinthians 15:41 says that "even the stars differ from each other in their beauty and brightness."

In his Word, God talks about gravity (Job 26:7; 38:31-33), the water cycle (Ecclesiastes 1:7; Isaiah 55:10), the effect of emotions on physical health (Proverbs 16:24 and 17:22), and even the control of cancer and heart disease (Leviticus 7:22-23 and 11:9, for example). This stuff was not on the top-ten, best-selling scroll list for 1000 B.C.!

The Bible tells us truths about our physical universe that could not be proven until modern science hit the scene. In the Bible we read truths about the spiritual universe, too. God, the Creator of the burning stars and the thundering oceans, wants to be our Father in heaven. To get a glimpse of what our absolutely awesome God is like, let's explore his absolutely awesome creation!

CORAL
Reefs

**And God said,
"Let the waters swarm
with fish and other life."**

Genesis 1:20

DAY 1: TEMPLES ON THE OCEAN FLOOR

Underwater wilderness with elkhorn coral in foreground.

Throughout history, people have built temples to honor their gods. The Babylonians assembled mountainlike ziggurats: tile-covered, mud-brick buildings that glistened in the desert sunlight. The Assyrians and Persians set up tall temples too. The biggest temples of all were the pyramids, built by the Egyptians to honor the dead kings they worshiped. The tallest pyramid was four hundred feet high, taller than a football field standing on end! Many of these cultures spent whole lifetimes making temples to reach into the sky as a tribute to their gods.

But those man-made temples are tiny compared to the amazing ocean monuments known as coral reefs. Coral reefs are stonelike rings around islands or near shores. The Great Barrier Reef off the coast of Australia stretches for 1,250 miles. In fact, all the coral reefs in the world put together cover as much of the earth as almost half of the United States! It would take a whole lifetime to learn everything about the zillion colorful sea creatures that make their homes in coral reef communities. Try that, Mr. Pharaoh, pyramid builder!

Coral is an animal, not a plant! A coral reef is built by tiny creatures called *coral polyps*. Just the size of a pea, coral polyps look like upside-down jellyfish. They are transparent and have tiny poison tentacles that capture microscopic creatures for food. Each polyp builds a stony house around its base. The house is made of limestone that the polyp makes from calcium carbonate in seawater. Calcium carbonate is the same stuff that other ocean creatures use to make seashells. When the polyp eventually dies, it leaves behind its skeleton house, called a *coralite,* and new polyps move in above it, making new coralites. Houses on top of houses of coralites form the magical towers and turrets of coral reefs. It's an oceanic condominium gone wild!

Scientists can count layers in the coral to estimate how old the reef is, just like they count the rings of a tree to find out its age. Some of the living coral reefs today are so thick that we know they were around at the time of the pyramids, thousands of years ago.

Unlike the soaring temples of the Babylonian kings and Egyptian pharaohs, coral reefs are living monuments to the God of all creation. These vast colonies of tiny creatures stand together to point to the designer of everything, a real God infinitely greater than all the gods people have invented for themselves. God's creation outshines anything that man can do! God is *the* creator.

Think about what God says to you

> *The God who made the world and*
> *everything in it is the Lord of heaven and earth and*
> *does not live in temples built by hands.*
> Acts 17:24, NIV

God created the marvelous natural wonders around us for his glory. Each thing he made tells us something about him. God wants us to look up into the sky and down into the ocean to see what he has made. As we find out more about all of his creation, we will learn to love him more, trust him more, and honor him more.

Let's talk to God!

MY JOURNAL

God, of all the things you have made, this one is the most amazing to me:

_____

because:

_____

_____

_____

_____

MY PRAYER

God, thank you for making the coral reefs as a reminder to me of your creative power and awesome glory. People can make beautiful, wonderful buildings, but they don't last. Your creation outlasts and outshines everything else.

The orange brain coral in the foreground feels like a rubber tire.

The first time you swim through a coral reef, you notice one thing: motion. Brightly colored fish flit by in the sunlight, while sea fans and grasses sway in the ocean currents.

The coral community is bursting with life. It's a good place to anchor for the tiny sea horses that hold onto the coral with their tails. It's a nursery for baby octopuses. They find it handy to hang out in the coral until they get big enough to live in the open sea by themselves. Sea cucumbers, giant blue clams, mandarin fish, strawberry shrimp, and hermit crabs all call the coral reef home sweet home.

If you go into a hobby store or shell shop and touch a dried sea fan, it will feel stiff and brittle. A dried piece of coral is as hard as rock. The life has gone out of it. But in a living coral reef, sea fans sway gracefully with the waves, bending and moving in a constant dance. That gray, stony brain coral in the shell shop was apricot orange and soft like a rubber tire when it was alive in the ocean.

Living things are full of color and movement. When these things are taken from their natural environment, they become cold and hard. God wants our faith to be a living thing, full of color and movement, like the creatures in a coral reef. When our relationship with God is distant, cold, and hard, our faith becomes old and dead.

5

This can happen if we are mad at God for a long time. It can also happen if we have tried to make him into the kind of God we think he should be instead of the God he really is. Jesus told the Pharisees that their faith in God had become cold and dead—he compared their faith to stony tombs.

But God wants us to have a faith that is alive and in motion. He wants us to wonder about him and his creation, to have questions, and to be flexible in our ideas about him—always checking, of course, to see that new ideas fit in with his Word. Our relationship with our Father in heaven can be as exciting and colorful as the wonderful creatures of the reef. The ocean is life to the creatures of the coral reef, and God is life to us. Our faith is a living thing, and to keep it alive we have to stay with the Life-giver!

Think about what God says to you

I will give you a new heart with new and right desires, and I will put a new spirit in you. I will take out your stony heart of sin and give you a new, obedient heart.
Ezekiel 36:26

When we have a close relationship with God, our lives are . . . *alive*. They aren't like that dried, hard brain coral, but like darting fish and graceful sea fans. When we dive into our relationship with God, we have energy, and it's a joy to be alive!

Let's talk to God!

MY JOURNAL

Acts 17:28 says, "In [God] we live and move and exist." This is how I would explain this verse in my own words :

_____

_____

_____

_____

MY PRAYER

Lord, you are like a life-giving ocean. When I am in a close relationship with you, I am really, truly alive. When I pull away from you, my faith starts to shrivel up and die. I want to always be with you. Please call me back if I start to wander away. I know that if I live my life in you, it will be a colorful and exciting adventure.

7

The colorful inhabitants of a coral reef swim up to greet author Caroline. We are guests in God's undersea gardens.

Coral reefs are the tropical rain forests of the ocean, filled with some of the most wacky, bizarre, and beautiful creatures around. The biggest, "baddest" reef of them all is the Great Barrier Reef off the coast of Australia. This down-under wonder is so long that it could stretch from New York to Kansas City. The Great Barrier Reef gets its name from being a natural breakwater, protecting Australia's northern coast from rough waves.

When you stand on the shore by the coral reef, all you see is blue-green water with dark shapes under the surface. But if you get your courage up, put on your diving mask, and jump into the water, a whole new world magically appears. There is so much beauty just under the surface. Life down there is exciting, riotous, and colorful. The corals build themselves into a fantastic wonderland of shapes. Brain coral, staghorn, elkhorn, flower coral, finger coral, tube coral, and even pillar coral all compete for your attention, along with gorgeous sea anemones and spiky sea urchins.

One out of every four ocean species lives in the reefs, so the reef is kind of like one big, interactive smorgasbord. The sea star eats the coral, and the triton conch eats the sea star. The Moorish idol fish eats the sponge, and the barracuda eats the Moorish idol fish. The octopus munches on the crab, and the Moray eel munches on the octopus. The green turtle eats the jellyfish, and the shark hunts the green turtle. There sure is a lot of action down there, and you would have missed it all if you hadn't dived in!

Some of the people we're around seem blah and unexciting on the surface. Perhaps you have a classmate or neighbor who seems boring—not worth getting to know. But God has made every person worthwhile and interesting in some way. Just like snorkeling in the Great Barrier Reef, it will take courage and hard work to explore. But it's a fun challenge to go beneath the surface and get to know the heart and mind of someone you don't know very well yet.

Think about what God says to you

> You look deep within the mind and heart,
> O righteous God.
>
> Psalm 7:9

If getting beneath the surface with people is important to God, it should be important to us also. So put on your face mask and dive in! Ask good questions and show an interest in the answers. If you are patient, God may show you something wonderful about the most shy, quiet, difficult-to-know person. You may even discover that, by looking below the surface, you have started to make a new friend.

Let's talk to God!

MY JOURNAL (choose one)

This is why I want to take the risk of getting beneath the surface with someone new:

_____

_____

_____

_____

This is one good question I could ask to help someone open up and talk to me:

_____

_____

_____

_____

MY PRAYER

Dear Lord, I want to confess that sometimes I just blow people off without ever thinking about the fact that you created them and gave them something to offer. I want to have the courage and take the time to reach out and get to know someone who is hard to know. Jesus took the time to look into the hearts and minds of everyone he met. Help me to do that too.

DAY 4: CLOWNING AROUND IN A DEADLY GARDEN

Elkhorn coral reaches toward the sun.

One of the most beautiful creatures in the coral reef is the flowerlike sea anemone. The sea anemone can be red, pink, or yellow. It sways in the currents washing over the reef, and its bright colors glow in the sunlight filtering down through the water. Growing out of the coral on a stalk, its graceful, petal-like tentacles are really poisonous arms waiting to catch and paralyze its next lunch. The sea anemone nabs tiny fish, shrimp, and other little creatures that swim by. Then the anemone's sticky tentacles pull the food into its mouth. Sushi!

Most fish like to keep their distance from the scary anemone, but not the clown fish. Only two inches long, this bright dude is decked out in orange and white stripes, and its habits are as bold as its color. Because of its wild coloring, the clown fish can't hide from its enemies. But thanks to a special coating on its skin, the clown fish hangs out, safe and sound, in the poisonous tentacles of the anemone. The coating that covers the fish is similar to the mucus that the anemone makes to protect itself from its own poison. Female clown fish even lay their eggs in the anemone's tentacles to protect them from getting eaten by other fish.

The tentacles of the sea anemone spell death to most small sea creatures. But the clown fish, with its special protective coating, finds safety, security, and life in the tentacles of the sea anemone. In the same way we Christians find protection and eternal life in God's hands. We have a special coating, too: it's the saving blood of Jesus Christ. God recognizes us as his own! We are protected from judgment and given the gift of eternal life.

Think about what God says to you

> *Godly people find life; evil people find death.*
> Proverbs 11:19

As Christians we've been saved and washed clean because of what Jesus did for us on the cross. We know we'll be alive with God in heaven forever when our lives here on earth are over. But it's different for non-Christians. They don't have a saving relationship with Jesus, so they don't receive the gift of eternal life.

Let's talk to God!

MY JOURNAL (choose one)
This is what I'd say to friends who don't think they need a protective coating from God:

_____

_____

_____

To show my thanks to Jesus Christ for his protective coating I will:

_____

_____

_____

MY PRAYER
Dear Lord, thank you so much for sending Jesus down to earth to cover my sins and to give me eternal life with you.

DAY 5: THE OCTOPUS— NO BONES ABOUT IT

The strange octopus has eight arms and blue blood. It can blend into its environment by changing color. (Photo courtesy Robert Patzner)

The octopus is unique among God's reef creatures. Sure, you know that an octopus has eight arms and a bag for a head. But did you know that:

- the octopus has blue blood? Our red blood has iron in it, but octopus blood has copper.
- the octopus has three hearts?
- instead of a round pupil, the octopus peers out through a horizontal slit?
- the octopus has no bones, but it does have a beak?
- the octopus turns bright red when it is angry and can change into many other colors, splotches, and stripes to blend in with its environment? Even baby octopuses still in their clear eggs change color.
- the octopus is as smart as a dog?

The octopus is shy, timid, and very intelligent. It is a member of the class *Cephalopoda,* which means "head-footed." It's a good name, isn't it? Even without a skeleton, it is strong. A large octopus can pull as much as six hundred pounds through the water! It keeps changing shape as it pulls itself along with its arms or jets through the sea using a stream of water shot through a hole in one side of its head. The average octopus is less than two feet across with a head the size of a grapefruit, but the largest octopus ever found had arms that stretched thirty-one feet from tip to tip. Basketball, anyone?

This "well-armed" creature can solve complex problems. In laboratory tests, when given a jar with a crab inside, the octopus can figure out how to open the jar. An octopus can solve mazes and recognize objects by touch.

Seals, sea lions, eels, and sharks all hunt octopus. But God has given the octopus a way out of dangerous situations. And the octopus is smart enough to use it. When attacked, it squirts a cloud of smelly black ink into the water—kind of like a "skunk of the sea"! Then the octopus changes color and direction, swimming away from danger. The attacker sees a dark shape but suddenly finds itself in a stinky, disorienting cloud. Unable to see or smell the octopus, the frustrated predator leaves in confusion!

We can learn from the octopus how to deal with dangers and temptations. When we're tempted, God always gives us a way out, just like that cloud of ink. Satan prowls "like a roaring lion" (1 Peter 5:8), seeking to do us harm; he is the one who tempts us, hoping we'll fail. God allows us to be tempted and tested, but he also always offers us the help we need to pass the tests.

Think about what God says to you

God is faithful. He will keep the temptation from becoming so strong that you can't stand up against it. When you are tempted, he will show you a way out so that you will not give in to it.
1 Corinthians 10:13

The Bible says *"when* you are tempted," not *"if* you are tempted." That means *everybody* gets tempted, so don't feel alone. It's just a matter of time before temptation comes along. It can take you by surprise, so you need to be ready to figure out what to do when it happens.

14

Here are some helpful tools from God's instruction manual—your own "stinky black clouds" to help you escape the dangers of temptation!

1. Find a friend who loves God and can help you choose to do the right things. (Proverbs 12:26; 13:20)
2. Stay away from tempting places and people. (Proverbs 1:10-15)
3. Run from any situation that tempts you. (1 Timothy 6:11)
4. Pray for God's awesome power to help you. (Matthew 6:13)
5. Follow Jesus' example and quote Scripture when Satan tempts you. (Matthew 4:4, 7, 10)

Let's talk to God!

MY JOURNAL (choose one)

God, you gave me a brain, so I'll use it! I'll learn which people and places tempt me to do wrong things, and I WON'T GO THERE. I need to stay away from:

_____

_____

_____

_____

Just like my friend the octopus, I must be smart enough to know when to leave a situation. I need to run if something like this happens:

_____

_____

_____

_____

MY PRAYER

Lord, please help me to use the intelligence you've given me just as the octopus uses the skills and abilities you've given it. You provide a way out for me when I am tempted, and I need to be smart enough to use it. When something comes along that I want to do but know I shouldn't, help me put up that cloud and swim the other way.

Experiment: The Underwater Oxygen Factory

The sea grasses and other plants living underwater in coral reefs are like plants everywhere on earth—they make oxygen. To prove that plants make oxygen even underwater, here's a quick and easy experiment to try.

FOR THIS EXPERIMENT YOU WILL NEED:

- a fresh leaf of lettuce from the garden or the fridge
- an empty glass jar
- a big glass bowl
- a small piece of cardboard

1. Fill half of the glass bowl with water.
2. Fill the glass jar almost to the top with water, and put the lettuce in the jar.
3. Cover the top of the jar with the cardboard
4. While holding the cardboard over the jar opening, turn the jar upside down and set it down in the glass bowl.
5. Gently slide the (wet!) cardboard out from under the jar.
6. Check to make sure the water and lettuce are high up inside the jar.
7. Set the bowl and jar in the sunlight, and wait two hours.
8. Check for bubbles appearing inside the jar with the lettuce. Those bubbles are oxygen!

Caring for God's Underwater World

Underwater plants make oxygen for our world, and they are an important part of God's plan to keep our planet "livable." Corals need clean, clear, oxygen-rich water to live in. Unfortunately, human pollution in the ocean is killing some of the coral reefs, and corals are now on the endangered species list. Coral collectors also hurt the reefs by breaking off chunks of coral to sell in stores. Some fishermen who poach the fish living in the coral reefs use a method called cyanide poison fishing, dropping poison tablets in the water and waiting for the dying fish to float to the surface. Others do blast fishing—a charge is detonated underwater, and the stunned fish float to the surface. Such fishing methods destroy the delicate balance of these special underwater communities. It's important for humans to take better care of the coral reefs around the world. Why? First, just because God tells us to care for his world, and second, because a healthy ocean means a healthy world for us to live in!

RAIN
Forests

He is like the light
of the morning, . . .
like the refreshing
rains that bring
tender grass
from the earth.

2 Samuel 23:4

*Rain forests spread across South
and Central America, covering
ancient ruins of the Mayan and
Aztec people.*

Life thrives in the canopy of the rain forest.

Tropical rain forests are hot, humid, and bursting with life. They swarm with spider monkeys and salamanders, ocelots and okapis, snakes and sloths, parrots and peccaries! These forests are home to half the animal and plant species on Earth, but they cover only 7 percent of the earth's land surface. In fact, nearly half of the world's animal species live in the canopy, or tops, of the trees. There are 30 million types of insects in these steamy jungles. Tropical rain forests are found in more than forty countries. The biggest rain forests are in Zaire, Indonesia, and Brazil.

"Tropical rain forest" is just the scientific name for jungle: a sweltering, steamy place where winter never comes. "Tropical" means near the equator, the part of our world that gets the most sunlight. The sun's rays hit the equator straight on, but they hit the rest of the earth at an angle, as Earth's surface curves away from the rays. So now we know why the rain forests are so hot.

But why are rain forests so wet? In most rain forests, it rains more than two hundred days per year! Much of this rain is recycled from the leaves of the trees. The trees clean the air, providing oxygen and moisture. Great air currents build up over the forests and carry the fresh air with them. Tropical rain forests are Earth's air-fresheners!

When God made the rain forests, he planned them in relationship with everything else he created. Rain forests provide moisture and warmth to the rest of the earth. But people who live in the rain forest countries are cutting down and burning rain forests at the rate of 50 million acres per year. They are destroying thousand-year-old jungles for logging and farming, but the soil is poor and supports farming only for a few years. Then they have nothing. They have traded the long-term benefits of the rain forest for a few years of crops. When a rain forest is destroyed, it affects the whole world. Carbon dioxide is released by the fires, but there are no trees to take it back in and breathe oxygen and water into the air.

Sometimes we have a relationship that has taken years to build up. If we destroy it with selfishness and sin, it is like burning a rain forest. We find out that we've ended up with nothing but a big mess. It will take a long time to grow that relationship back again, if it can grow back at all.

Think about what God says to you

*There are "friends" who destroy each other,
but a real friend sticks closer than a brother.*
Proverbs 18:24

Sometimes it's tempting to get what you want even though it hurts someone else. You might feel like lying to your parents so you can go do something they have forbidden. You might think about fooling your teacher by cheating on a test that you didn't get around to studying for. You might be tempted to turn against your friend so you can be more popular with the cool crowd. But don't do it! Getting what you want isn't worth destroying a relationship.

Let's talk to God!

MY JOURNAL (choose one)

This is one time I did something that hurt my parents, my teacher, or my friend:

_____

_____

_____

_____

This is what it did to our relationship:

_____

_____

_____

_____

This is what I will do the next time I'm tempted to turn against a friend:

_____

_____

_____

_____

MY PRAYER

Dear God, your Word talks about you when it says, "He is a God who is passionate about his relationship with you" (Exodus 34:14). Thank you for being passionate about your relationship with me! Thank you for taking it seriously. Please give me the wisdom to take my relationships seriously. Please give me the strength not to risk my relationships here on Earth by being selfish and sinful.

The waters of the dark Rio Negro meet the milky waters of the Rio Solimões to form the mighty Amazon River.

The Amazon River runs through the tropical rain forests of South America. It is the largest river in the world—20 percent of the freshwater on Earth flows through it each day. The Amazon's flow is more powerful than the world's eight next biggest rivers put together! Every year it floods its banks, which brings nutrients to the rain forest soil.

Two smaller rivers, the Rio Negro ("Black River") and the Rio Solimões, join together to make the mighty Amazon. The Rio Negro begins in Venezuela and has water as dark as black coffee. The river is black because it has tree bark and dead plants in it that are high in the acid tannin. If you stand knee-deep in the waters of the Rio Negro, you won't see your feet!

The Rio Solimões has water that is a light, milky brown tinted by silt from the Andes Mountains. The place where the two rivers meet is remarkable. Six miles below the jungle town of Manaus, Brazil, the black waters of the Rio Negro flow into a wide waterway. There the dark waters are met by the lighter waters of the Solimões, and the two become the Amazon River. For miles and miles the two waters will not mix. A boat going down the Amazon can literally travel with black water on one side of the boat and light water on the other side. The waters do not mix because of the acid in the Rio Negro and the greater thickness (density) of the water in the Rio Solimões.

Just as the milky water of the Rio Solimões will not mix with the black waters of the Rio Negro, God's perfect, pure holiness will not let him mix with the darkness of our sin. And let's face it—none of us is perfect. We've all done things that go against God's commands. God's Son, Jesus, who led a perfect and pure life, has paid the price for our sin. So when God looks at us, he doesn't see our sin. Because of Jesus' death on the cross, God calls us his children, and his Spirit flows into us. Wow! What a great thing God has done for us by sending us his Son. Instead of being a dark little river on our own, we can become part of his powerful river when he cleanses us!

Think about what God says to you

Your eyes are too pure to look on evil; you cannot tolerate wrong.
Habakkuk 1:13, NIV

God is so pure that he is never in a place where there is sin. Although the children of God are not perfect, Christ has taken on our sin so that God sees only the perfection and holiness of Jesus when he looks at us. Thanks to Jesus, imperfect people like you and me can be in the presence of God and be filled with his Spirit.

Let's talk to God!

MY JOURNAL (choose one)
God, this is why I think you would never be in the presence of sin:

_____

_____

_____

_____

Thinking about the Amazon River will help me avoid sin when I'm tempted because:

_____

_____

_____

_____

MY PRAYER

Dear God, you and sin cannot live in the same space. But even though I have sin in my life, I am so happy that Jesus has washed it away. Now when you see me, you see me all fresh and clean.

The jaguar is one of many species that is disappearing rapidly.

The Amazon rain forest is a fascinating ecosystem. Here are some things you might see during a typical day deep in the Amazon. Giant six-foot-long otters, the rarest of rain forest animals, splash in the river, avoiding the hungry caimans (similar to crocodiles) and anaconda snakes. A one-thousand-pound manatee munches on water lilies as freshwater dolphins play nearby. A jaguar prowls along the riverbank, stalking a forest deer. A tapir, the largest mammal in the Americas, crashes through the brush. Up in the treetops a tiny hummingbird sits in her thimble-sized nest, incubating eggs the size of coffee beans, and a howler monkey feasts on ripe fruit.

But what would you see on a typical night in the Amazon? As the daytime creatures bed down for the evening, the nocturnal animals take their place in the darkness. With night-vision goggles and a thermos of iced tea to keep you awake, this is what you might see. The red-eyed tree frog appears for its nightly snack of bugs. The *douroucouli*, or night monkey, moves gracefully through the trees. It has enormous eyes and is the only nocturnal monkey known. It eats leaves, fruit, bugs, and small animals. The spotted margay, a small cat related to the ocelot, silently climbs down a huge tree. The spotted margay's hind feet turn backwards so it can descend trees headfirst!

Suddenly, something flutters by your head. You jump. Aren't all the birds asleep up in the trees? Yep. You just met a bat. Almost half of the mammal species in the Amazon rain forest are bats. Bats are the only true flying mammal that God has

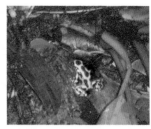

The poison arrow frog wears the colors of the world around him.

made, and they are specially designed to fly at night. The cooler air brings the insects out, and the hunting is good. The only problem is that the insects are hard to see. So many bats of the Amazon fly by *echolocation*, or sonar. The bat gives very fast, high-pitched squeaks. These sounds echo off any nearby object and come back to the bat's large ears, giving the bat information about the size, shape, and distance of the object. Thanks to sonar, the bat can fly with confidence and catch insects even in the blackest of jungle nights.

Just as God gave the bat sonar for navigating in pitch darkness, he has given us something special as well. He has given us a spiritual gift to guide us through this sometimes dark world. That gift is faith.

Think about what God says to you

> *We know that when this earthly tent we live in is taken down—when we die and leave these bodies—we will have a home in heaven, an eternal body made for us by God himself and not by human hands....*
> *That is why we live by believing and not by seeing.*
> 2 Corinthians 5:1, 7

Have you ever heard the words, "Walk by faith, not by sight"? That comes from 2 Corinthians 5:7, KJV. If we just use our human eyes to lead us along in this world, we will get lost and confused. The world can seem like a scary place if we look only at what we see in the newspaper and on TV. But God tells us to walk by our faith—to live by believing in him and his promises. This gives us confidence and peace, helping us to serve God faithfully while we are here on Earth.

Let's talk to God!

MY JOURNAL (choose one)

This is how I will try to live by believing and not by seeing:

_____

_____

_____

_____

When I remember that heaven is my true home, I feel:

_____

_____

_____

_____

MY PRAYER

Dear Lord, I am so glad to know that I have an eternal home with you in heaven. I will live my life believing faithfully in you and in all that you tell me in the Bible.

Rain forests have more species per square foot than any other ecosystem, but both the forests and the creatures in them are disappearing fast. Here is a list of some endangered rain forest creatures: the South American river turtle, the Amazon River dolphin, the jaguar, the yellow spotted tree frog, the Asian elephant, the proboscis monkey, the orangutan, the pygmy chimpanzee, and the Borneo peacock-pheasant.

Also endangered are God's magnificent mountain gorillas of the African rain forest. Although they have a fierce reputation, they are very gentle giants. The mountain gorillas live in peaceful groups of between five and thirty animals. They are led by a dominant silverback male that can be up to six feet tall and weigh 350 pounds. Female mountain gorillas are half that size. Gorilla babies weigh about five pounds at birth and sleep in their mothers' nests until they are three years old. Even the silverback males are gentle and patient with the babies.

Mountain gorillas spend their days browsing for food, playing, and dozing in the sun. Gorillas are vegetarians. They eat fruit, leaves, bark, stems, roots, vines, bamboo, wild cherries, wild celery, thistles, and nettles. They spend most of the day on the ground, unless there is a tree with ripe fruit nearby. Then, if the tree is strong enough to hold them, they climb up to feast on the fruit. At night, for a good night's sleep, they climb into the trees where they have built their nests.

As of the writing of this book, there are only 325 mountain gorillas left in the world. They live in a small wedge of rain forest surrounded by growing human populations. Loss of habitat, poaching, and recent civil wars have caused the mountain gorilla to be placed on the "critically endangered species" list. Refugees from the wars have moved into the mountains, chopping down the forest for farming, and hunting the gorillas for food.

Think about what God says to you

God blessed them and told them, "... Be masters over the fish and birds and all the animals."
Genesis 1:28

The earth belongs to God. He created all the mountains, rivers, plants, and animals with a great deal of love and thought. He has given us the job of taking good care of our planet. He wants us to be good stewards of everything he has made, which means it's important not to be wasteful and destructive.

Let's talk to God!

MY JOURNAL

This is one way I can help one of your creatures, God:

_____

_____

_____

_____

MY PRAYER

Dear God, you created each animal for a reason. I will care for your creatures as best I can, and I will try to be a good steward of all that you have made.

The mighty sequoia is the most mega tree on planet Earth.

Did you know we have rain forests here in the United States? Not all rain forests are in tropical places. There are cool rain forests that get just as much rainfall as the tropical ones do, but they contain different kinds of plants, trees, and animals. These are called *temperate rain forests*. Temperate rain forests are sprinkled from the coast of northern California up to southern Alaska.

Redwood trees, known by scientists as sequoias, are the largest trees on Earth. They live only in a narrow strip along the rainy coasts of northern California and southern Oregon. Some live in our temperate rain forests. They have needlelike leaves and strong wood that doesn't rot. Because of this, redwood is used for outdoor building materials, like shingles and decks. Some redwoods grow up to 380 feet high and are so big around that a tunnel was made in one to let cars drive through!

Several years ago one of the larger redwoods in northern California fell over. There was no wind, and the outside of the tree looked strong. But when scientists looked inside the tree, they found thousands of tiny tunnels eaten through by beetles. The giant tree fell because of a tiny insect. Many of the redwoods are infested by beetles. Usually a tree remains strong if there are only a few beetle tunnels in

32

it. But if enough of the little beetles get in, the strong tree becomes hollow inside and eventually falls.

There are many things in life that we know we should not do. We tend to think that if we do just one little wrong thing, it won't hurt us. But the truth is that little things—a little lie here or a tiny cheat there—can cause our spiritual tree trunk to become riddled with "beetle tunnels." The disease of sin takes hold, and before we know it there is sin all through us that makes us weak and miserable.

Only God can fill those "beetle tunnels" back in to make us strong again.

Think about what God says to you

He forgives all my sins and heals all my diseases.
Psalm 103:3

God can heal our diseases, including the disease of sin, and make us whole if we ask him to. But God wants us to avoid life's little beetles in the first place so that we can live strong, happy lives in his power.

Let's talk to God!

MY JOURNAL (choose one)

In today's story about the redwood, I think the redwood represents:

_____

_____

_____

_____

and the beetles represent:

_____

_____

_____

_____

God, this is a "beetle" that I need you to help me with so it doesn't start digging harmful tunnels that make me miserable:

_____

_____

_____

_____

MY PRAYER

Jesus, you have made life a wonderful thing. There are many good things to do, but sometimes I get caught up in things that are not so good. Like the beetles hurt the redwoods, I know that sin will hurt me. Help me to be strong so that when I am faced with a decision, I will do the right thing. Thank you, Jesus, for forgiving me and healing me from sin.

Experiment: How Plants Drink Water

PART 1

1. Ask your mom or dad if you can use some red food coloring and a stalk of celery with the leaves still on it. It's best to use one of the palest, inside stalks for this experiment.
2. Fill a glass one-fourth full with water, then add ten drops of red food coloring.
3. Trim the end off the celery stalk with a pair of scissors, and put the stalk in the water.
4. Check on the leaves whenever you think of it for the next two days. What happens?

PART 2

After two days you will have seen that plants absorb water through their roots and stems. The water is then carried up to the leaves. You can't see this on the outer stem because it happens inside the stem. Let's check it out. You'll need a magnifying glass for this part.

1. Take the celery out of the water and cut about an inch off the bottom of the celery stalk.
2. Look at the cross-section of the stalk. What do you see? Examine the tiny red tubes with your magnifying glass.

Experiment: The Rain Forest Water Cycle

Put a baggie over the leaves of a tree branch that's in the sun and twist-tie it. After an hour or so, check the baggie. What has happened?

You'll see that water has collected in the baggie. This water was sent out by the leaves. After the trees take in water through their roots, they release most of it back into the atmosphere. This is called *evapotranspiration.*

Activity: Rain Forest Products

Circle the items that are products of the rain forest.

African violets	Coca-Cola	nutmeg
bananas	coffee	peanuts
Brazil nuts	cooking oil	pineapples
chewing gum	ginger	soap
chocolate	hot cocoa	sugar
Christmas cactus	latex gloves	tapioca pudding
cinnamon	lemons	tea
cloves	margarine	

(Answer: all of the above!)

Now put an X over those items that you think are raised by farmers who have cleared and burned the rain forest to grow these crops.

(Answer: coffee, peanuts, sugar, tea)

JUPITER
The Big Kahuna

His Spirit made the heavens beautiful.

Job 26:13

If we could see electricity and magnetic fields, Jupiter would be a scary and beautiful place. The moon Io sails through a doughnut of electrified sodium gas. A sheet of electricity pours from the north and south poles of Io into Jupiter, pumping up the mighty planet's auroras on its poles as lightning flickers below Jupiter's clouds.

DAY 1: THE BIGGEST STORM AROUND

Two and one half Earths would fit inside the Great Red Spot, Jupiter's most powerful storm. (Galileo spacecraft photo courtesy NASA/JPL)

Jupiter is the biggest object in our solar system, besides our sun. It's a weather world with no solid surface. Through telescopes, we can see bands of clouds across Jupiter. These colorful bands swirl around the surface of this huge planet at hundreds of miles an hour. The bands are called *zones*, and they are bordered by dark belts. You wouldn't think anything could stay put on this windy world, but one storm has always been there—at least since people first invented telescopes that could see it. And it's a doozy.

The Great Red Spot is a storm so big that you could fit two and a half Earths across it. This wheeling cyclone spins around once every six days, gobbling up nearby storms that are the size of the United States. Winds at its edge roar along at 250 miles per hour. (If you lose your hat on Jupiter, kiss it good-bye!) The red color of the storm seems to be coming from below the visible clouds, where red and brown chemicals are made when lightning zaps through Jupiter's hydrogen, methane, and ammonia atmosphere.

The Great Red Spot is one of many storms. White oval cyclones the size of Earth's moon come and go in a matter of months or years. Bands of clouds blow in different directions, tearing at each other's edges and pulling off swirls and streamers of clouds.

Jupiter would be a stormy, miserable place to live. Do you know of any places like that? People can stir up storms too. If you have ever stirred up trouble, you know that you can make your own home a miserable place to live. Do you entertain yourself by mercilessly teasing your brother or sister? Do you argue with your parents just to make things interesting around home? Do you ever play "Let's make Mom mad"? Do you pick fights with your friends? When you stir up trouble, you create storms that disappoint God and your family. And, if you think about it, you probably feel disappointed with yourself too.

Think about what God says to you

Here is a description of worthless and wicked people: . . .
They stir up trouble constantly.
Proverbs 6:12,14

When we are tempted to stir up trouble, we need to remember that God calls that behavior "wicked." Let's be peacemakers instead. When we act as peacemakers, God promises we will be blessed.

Let's talk to God!

MY JOURNAL (choose one)
This is how I feel, God, when I stir up trouble at home:

_____

_____

_____

_____

Lord, I don't want to stir up trouble because:

_____

_____

_____

MY PRAYER

Dear God, if I'm absolutely honest, I have to admit that I stir up trouble sometimes, and I make my home a stormy place. I know that disappoints you and hurts my family. Please forgive me and show me how to do better.

The main ring of Jupiter seen nearly edge-on. Subtle structure can be seen in the glowing disk of material. (Galileo spacecraft photo courtesy NASA/JPL)

Any scientist can tell you that Jupiter is full of gas. But another thing the giant planet is full of is surprises! Weird moons, *mucho grande* lightning, and those way big storms all add to the flabbergast file. But there's another one. When the Voyager I spacecraft gave us our first clear view of the Jupiter system, it was programmed to look back toward the sun from Jupiter's night side. When it did, it discovered some beautiful golden rings around Jupiter. These rings are fainter than Saturn's rings, and our eyes can't even see them on the bright, sunlit side of the planet. But get around to the night side, and they appear. This is because the rings are made up of tiny, misty particles as fine as cigarette smoke. Jupiter's Main Ring is a disk of material that stretches seven thousand kilometers across space, but is only thirty kilometers thick. A faint Halo Ring is just inside the Main Ring, with a vast cloud of particles called the Gossamer Ring outside. Several of Jupiter's moons orbit within the rings, as we will see in Day 3.

The faint rings of Jupiter are beautiful, sparkling in the sunlight. But if the sky were not black behind them, we would never have spotted them. The contrast between light and dark lets us see the awesome radiance of the golden rings of Jupiter.

Sometimes life looks black, doesn't it? We argue with our friends and family, school doesn't go well, or we just don't feel that life is fair. But without those dark times, we could not understand how good God is to us. His blessings shine like the rings of Jupiter against the dark times in life. And when we really think about it, we see that those dark times don't last forever. But God's promises and blessings do!

Think about what God says to you

The people who sat in darkness have seen a great light. And for those who lived in the land where death casts its shadow, a light has shined.

Matthew 4:16

Jesus is called "a light to reveal God to the nations" (Luke 2:32). He wants to be our light in those times that seem dark. The Lord uses the dark times to show us how great his light and his blessings are.

Let's talk to God!

MY JOURNAL

This is something that happened this week that made my life feel dark:

_____

_____

_____

_____

God, this is someone or something that you have used to bring a bright spot into my life after a "dark day":

_____

_____

_____

_____

MY PRAYER

Dear Father, sometimes when things are tough, I concentrate on how bad things are and not on you. But if I look for you, you're right there. In fact, it's often easiest to see you when things look pretty dark.

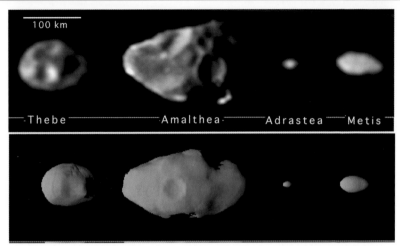

Some of the best views of Jupiter's small moons. From left: Metis, Andrastea, Amalthea, and Thebe. (Galileo spacecraft photo courtesy NASA/JPL)

How would you like to be able to jump a thousand times higher than you ever have? What would it be like to toss a baseball hundreds of miles or kick a soccer ball into orbit? There are at least twenty-two moons of Jupiter (and maybe more to be discovered), and if you lived on some of Jupiter's smallest moons, you could do all these things! These moons are nothing more than giant boulders circling Jupiter. As moons go, they're so small that they have very little gravity, so things don't "stick" to them as much as they do to the ground on Earth. If you trip and fall on the moon Amalthea, don't worry! You'll have half an hour before you hit the ground, and you won't even feel it!

The moons Metis and Andrastea are less than 40 miles across. They float right in the middle of Jupiter's Main Ring. Amalthea is much bigger—nearly 120 miles across. (It would take about six and a half hours to drive all the way around it on a highway if there was one, which there isn't. Not even a snack bar.) Amalthea clears a path through the Gossamer Ring. Outside of Amalthea orbits tiny Thebe, just 60 miles long. You could ride a bicycle from the north to the south pole of Thebe in a couple of days!

All of these moonlets are covered with craters from meteors smashing into them. Meteors come in all sizes, but the tiniest meteors, called *micrometeorites,* are smaller than a grain of sand. They rain steadily onto the moons like a gentle drizzle. When these mini-meteors hit, they kick up dust from the moons that drifts away in the low gravity. What happens to the dust? It becomes the amazing rings of Jupiter!

Over a long period of time, tiny impacts from micrometeorites smooth out the rough, rocky landscapes of Jupiter's minimoons. With each hit, another bit of dust goes into the sky to brighten the Gossamer and Main rings. Each hit knocks off sharp edges, sculpting the moons into something more graceful.

Life sends micrometeorites our way, too! Small things can aggravate us or get in the way of our plans. But if we handle the small things well, they can sculpt us into more graceful people, able to take the pressures of life like champs. God uses the micrometeorites of life to knock off our rough edges and to polish us so that we can shine with his light.

Think about what God says to you

> *Lord, you are our Father. We are the clay, and you are the potter. We are all formed by your hand.*
>
> Isaiah 64:8

God our Father shapes us just as a potter shapes clay. He uses all our experiences, big and small, to shape us. He knocks off our rough edges so that we grow to look more and more like Jesus in the way we speak, the way we act, and the way we live.

Let's talk to God!

MY JOURNAL

This is a big thing in my life that God is using to change me:

_____

_____

_____

_____

This is a little thing in my life that God is using to change me:

_____

_____

_____

_____

MY PRAYER

God, I know you are using events in my life to "knock off" my sharp edges and smooth me into the person you want me to be. But sometimes it's hard to see things that way. Help me to be patient with those around me who bother me, or with events in my life that seem too much to handle. Help me always to keep in mind that you are using all the happenings in my life to make me more like Jesus. I know it will take a lifetime. Thank you, Lord, for loving me enough to spend so much time smoothing me out!

DAY 4: THE SUPERCHARGED ELECTRIC MOON

Jupiter's mysterious moon Io is battered by volcanic splotches and powerful electric fields that flow between it and Jupiter.

Three days ago we discussed the great storms of Jupiter, with their flashing lightning and wicked winds. But there's an even more powerful force on Jupiter that you can't see. Deep inside the planet, liquid metal swirls around, acting like a mega-magnet. Its super-strong magnetic fields sweep around Jupiter through space at lightning speed. As they pass over Jupiter's volcanic moon, Io, something really outrageous happens.

You may recall from *Absolutely Awesome I* how weird Io is, with its pizza-colored face and giant volcanoes. But Io gets "Weirdest Moon of the Year" award once again for this: Io's volcanoes pour out tons of tiny particles every second. As Io circles Jupiter, these particles become a giant donut, with Jupiter as the gooey center. As Jupiter's magnetic fields pass through this donut, they charge it up with 5 million amps of electricity. (That's one million TV sets going full blast.) But that's just the shocking beginning. A sheet of electrical current known as the flux tube forms a sort of electrical short-circuit between Io and Jupiter. The electricity that flows from Jupiter to Io is 400,000 volts. (That's 3,333 times as much electricity as is coursing through your house right now!)

Jupiter is the powerful energy source that sets up fields of electricity, and Io pumps up those fields with its volcanoes. Guess what—that's a lot like our relationship with God! He is our source of spiritual power. He gives power to us, and we give our own energy and time back to him. In this way his power first flows *to* us, and then it flows out again *from* us.

Think about what God says to you

> *May you experience the love of Christ, though it is so great you will never fully understand it. Then you will be filled with the fullness of life and power that comes from God.*
> *Ephesians 3:19*

As we get to know God better, we see him as our source of strength and power. Just as Jupiter's power energizes Io, God's power energizes us, giving us the strength we need. What happens if we try to heat something in a microwave that's unplugged? Nothing! That's why we need to stay "plugged in" to God. He is our power source, and without him nothing good can happen.

Let's talk to God!

MY JOURNAL (choose one)

One time your power gave me strength, God, was when:

_____

_____

_____

_____

I think I'm really going to need your power, God, to help me with this:

_____

_____

_____

_____

MY PRAYER

Dear Father, thank you, thank you, thank you for being all-powerful. I am weak, but you are strong enough for both of us. You give me the strength I need each day because you love me so much. You give me the power to speak up for you and tell others your Good News. You give me the power to forgive people who have hurt me. You give me the power to do your work in a world that doesn't understand you.

DAY 5: RAISIN MOON

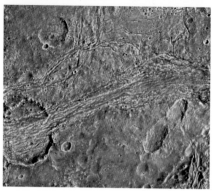

The strange stripes, valleys, and other land forms give scientists an idea of what is below Ganymede's surface. (Galileo spacecraft photo courtesy NASA/JPL)

What has more wrinkles than a raisin, is colder than an ice cube, and is bigger than a planet? The answer, of course, is Jupiter's largest moon, Ganymede. You knew that, right? (Maybe you recall reading about this moon in *Absolutely Awesome I*.)

Ganymede is larger than the planet Mercury and stranger than your brain can imagine. Spacecraft have shown us a tortured, twisted surface of troughs, furrows, valleys, and long strings of mountains. This planet-moon looks like somebody took a giant fork and scraped its surface.

What's with this icy moon? Deep inside lies the answer. Ganymede has an iron core covered by water. Most of this water is ice. But under the frozen crust lies a deep ocean of slush or liquid. Like Jupiter, Ganymede has a magnetic field, but it is so weak that no one knew about it until the robot spacecraft *Galileo* flew right through it. The magnetic field that *Galileo* recorded is similar to one that is driven by an ocean. The ocean under Ganymede's surface is kept warm and wet by the tug of gravity from Jupiter and two nearby moons, Europa and Callisto. The cosmic tug of war heats the interior of Ganymede. With a soft inside, the surface of Ganymede can be sculpted by the forces of nature that God has placed around Jupiter: energy fields, gravity, and meteors. The way Ganymede responds to these things tells scientists what's beneath the surface.

The important thing to remember is that the outside of Ganymede is the way it is because of what's inside of Ganymede. What is on the inside affects what is on the outside, from wrinkly ridges to magnetic fields. We are like that too. What is inside of us determines how we act on the outside. If we are filled with the Spirit of God on the inside, we will be more like Jesus on the outside.

Think about what God says to you

This precious treasure—this light and power that now shine within us—is held in perishable containers, that is, in our weak bodies. So everyone can see that our glorious power is from God and is not our own.

2 Corinthians 4:7

It is the Holy Spirit inside of us, shining out, that counts. The way we handle life will show people that the Holy Spirit lives in us. Sure, we'll have bad days like anyone else. But with God's help, we can handle those bad days differently than people who don't have the comforting Spirit inside of them. We'll be kind, gentle, and loving.

Let's talk to God!

MY JOURNAL (choose one)

This was one time when your Holy Spirit inside me changed how I handled things on the outside:

_____

_____

_____

_____

Galatians 2:20 says, "I myself no longer live, but Christ lives in me." When I put this verse into my own words it means:

_____

_____

_____

_____

MY PRAYER

Dear God, you fill me up on the inside with the comfort and wisdom of your Holy Spirit. I know I won't handle things well on the outside every time, but that's okay. With the Holy Spirit's help, I'll handle things much better than I would have on my own, and I'll be more like Jesus.

Putting the Spotlight on Jupiter's Ring

Here is a fun and easy way to figure out why Jupiter's ring shines:

1. Gather a flashlight and some baby powder.
2. Go into a darkened room—maybe the garage or a bathroom with no window.
3. Turn on the flashlight and set it on the edge of a table on its side.
4. Hold the bottle of baby powder under the beam of light and give it a good squeeze.

What happens? The light path from the flashlight is easy to see when the baby powder is floating around in it, right? Why? We can't see light unless it is reflected back to our eyes by some object. The little particles of baby powder act just like the tiny specks of particles that ring Jupiter. The flashlight acts just like the sun.

Notice, too, that when the baby powder is between you and the flashlight, the floating particles in the beam are even brighter. This is because small particles scatter light backward, away from the sun (or the flashlight) and toward your eyes. Because of this, Jupiter's rings are nearly invisible when we are on the same side as the sun, but they seem brighter when the sun is behind them

CHILLING OUT
in the Ice Age

God's breath sends the ice, freezing wide expanses of water.

Job 37:10

DAY 1: WATCH OUT FOR THE GIANT CREEPING ICE CUBE!

Glaciers like this one covered much of North America during the last ice age.

The Tlingit Indians of Alaska call glaciers "ice mountains," but glaciers are huge, happenin' ice cubes that do a whole lot more moving around than any mountain. Glaciers look like frozen, layered mountain slopes, but they are really creeping rivers of ice, slowly grinding their way down the sides of mountains and gouging out valleys. Glaciers contain mysterious microbes, frozen fossils, and clues to past lifestyles of people and animals. They are ancient and have left their marks all over the world, even in a few places that are now hot deserts and jungles.

Glaciers exist today in cold parts of the world, but during the Ice Age they were the big thing worldwide. Glaciers covered nearly a third of the earth's land mass. The ice sheets that covered North America were ten thousand feet thick, as high as a small plane flies! Today's tallest buildings would have been buried deep within these cool and crazy ice sheets.

What we call the Ice Age was really a series of ice ages broken up by warmer periods of time. The snazzy scientific term for the Ice Age is the *Pleistocene Epoch*. Forests disappeared underneath massive walls of ice that moved across the landscape. Then, as the earth warmed, the huge glaciers melted. In their places they left behind grasslands as beautiful as the forests, but very different. Gone were the trees and woodland animals. Instead, the land was filled with bright tundra flowers, grassy plains, and new kinds of grazing creatures. Eventually forests grew up again. Then the cold returned, bringing glaciers and wiping out the grassy plains and new forests.

Times were very tough for people and animals during the ice ages. The climate would be warm for a long period of time, then another ice age would suddenly begin. They had to change and adapt, or die. In the same way, we as Christians need to adapt spiritually to the changing seasons in our lives. For some reason, God has designed us so that we do our best spiritual growing and changing during the difficult times, when we are moved out of our comfort zones and into new situations.

Think about what God says to you

I will . . . transform the Valley of Trouble into a gateway of hope.
Hosea 2:15

Sometimes it feels like we are being crushed under the pressure of ten thousand feet of ice. When the pressure is gone, we are changed forever. We feel different. God has used a difficult time of change to help us grow in our relationship with him.

MY JOURNAL (choose one)

God, I think you use difficult times to help us grow because:

_____

_____

_____

_____

Lord, hard times either move me closer to you or farther away from you. I want to move closer to you when:

_____

_____

_____

_____

MY PRAYER

Lord, sometimes it seems as though I'm going through my own "Ice Age." Help me to adapt and adjust and become more like Jesus in the tough times.

Find Out More: Excellent Ice Age Web Sites

La Brea Tar Pits (Los Angeles, California)
>   www.tarpits.org

Mammoth Site (Hot Springs, South Dakota)
>   www.mammothsite.com

DAY 2: BRIDGE BETWEEN TWO WORLDS

This ocean hides Beringia, the great land bridge that once connected Asia with North America.

There is a very shallow place in the sea between what's now Alaska and Siberia. When the world had a cold snap for a few thousand years, many glaciers formed. Because so much of the world's water was ice, the oceans were three hundred feet lower back then! We can actually see ancient shore lines underwater today.

When the oceans were lower, Siberia and Alaska were connected, and this vast land area was called Beringia, or the Bering land bridge. This area was a bridge on which the creatures that lived in Asia and Europe could come over to a new place. And a wonderful place it was! Ancient America had camels and lions and other critters that we don't normally think of as living on this continent.

And it appears that many people came over the land bridge as well. God started his people in Eden (somewhere in the Middle East or Africa), and they had to get to America somehow. After all, he told Adam and Eve to "multiply and fill the earth" (Genesis 1:28). Thanks to the Ice Age, with its lowering of the oceans, God enabled people to go all over the world. God used the ancient land bridge that is now hidden from us to bring people to a new continent to "fill the earth." Scientists believe people either followed the coastline of Beringia to America in boats, or they came by land over Beringia's rolling plains, following mammoths and other animals they hunted. Whatever the method, they arrived in the New World and made new lives there.

59

During the Ice Age, people left their old lives and crossed the land bridge to begin new lives in the New World. In Exodus, God opened up a path through the water for Moses and the escaping Israelites. On one side of the water was death—the Egyptians were after them! On the other side of the water was new life in the Promised Land— a place to rest in the great promises of God. Then, in the New Testament, we learn how God sent his own Son to bridge the gap between himself and us. As always, God continues to make a way for his people to come to him.

Think about what God says to you

> There is only one God and one Mediator who can reconcile God and people. He is the man Christ Jesus. He gave his life to purchase freedom for everyone.
>
> I Timothy 2:5-6

Jesus is like a bridge between people, who are sinful, and God, who is holy. A father who wanted to teach this point to his two little girls had them stand on one side of a stream near their home. It was too wide to jump over and had no fallen logs or stones to step on. He stood on the other side, and said, "Do you think you can cross over to my side of the stream without getting wet?" "Yes!" they shouted, but in a few minutes they had tried everything they could think of and couldn't figure out how to do it. "Give up?" their dad asked. "Yes!" they said. So their father crossed the stream, picked them both up in his strong arms, and carried them across to the other side.

Let's talk to God!

MY JOURNAL (choose one)

Lord, this is why I think you planned it so we can't make it to heaven on our own power:

_____

_____

_____

_____

Lord, this is how I understand Jesus is like a bridge:

_____

_____

_____

_____

MY PRAYER

God, you sent Jesus to be the bridge between me and you. Help me understand that I can never get to heaven on my own. I need you to provide the way. Thank you, Jesus, for being my bridge, for coming to earth as a human so that I can be a child of God.

· ·

Extinction Theories

Many of the huge animals that inhabited North and South America during the Ice Age became extinct in a short period of time. What caused this extinction? Two popular theories both involve humans. One theory is that the humans hunted the animals until they were all gone. The other theory is that humans brought germs with them over the land bridge that infected and killed the animals. Other theories may come along, but we may never know what killed off the mammoth and his buddies.

· ·

DAY 3: LIONS AND CAMELS AND BEARS, OH MY!

A five-hundred-foot-high wall of glacial ice stretched from what is now Seattle to New York.

Thousands of years ago, when North America looked a lot like the African plains, it was complete with lions, rhinos, and other strange creatures. A blanket of ice two miles thick covered the top half of North America, as well as much of Europe and Asia. The southern edge of these glaciers ended in a 500-foot-high ice cliff that stretched from what is now Seattle to Chicago to New York. To the south of these great ice sheets grew grassy plains and deep forests.

This land was filled with fascinating creatures, truly some of the most astounding animals that God ever created. Enormous carnivores, or meat-eaters, roamed this ancient world. Most were built on a much bigger scale than the North American wildlife of today. The giant short-faced bear would make our grizzly bear look like a golden retriever. *Smilodon,* the fearsome ten-foot-long saber-toothed tiger, had six-inch-long, daggerlike canine teeth. It used these teeth for stabbing its victims and then slashing the jugular veins in their necks.

Smilodon had plenty of prey animals to hunt. Across the plains of this Ice Age world thundered

herds of prehistoric woolly rhinoceroses with fan-shaped horns on their noses. Other creatures that looked like short-necked giraffes had four horns and long tusks. Irish elk had antlers eleven feet across! These hooved plant-eaters were called *ungulates*. Today's ungulates include all large, plant-eating mammals except elephants.

And speaking of *big*—swimming in the lakes and rivers were giant beavers seven feet long, weighing as much as three seventh-graders! Some of these cool creatures had armored skin. *Glyptodonts* had clubbed tails much like some dinosaurs did. Some were so huge that the ancient people of South America used their shells for huts! One of the weirdest woollies was the giant ground sloth. It was as large as an elephant, with hidden, bony pebbles of armor under its thick fur.

As the climate changed, many of the ice-age animals became extinct, but a few are still around today, looking exactly as they did thousands of years ago. They include caribou, bison, antelope, polar bears, and musk ox. When we look at those creatures, we get a glimpse of the magnificence of God's creatures of the Ice Age.

Think about what God says to you

> *See its powerful loins and the muscles of its belly.*
> *Its tail is as straight as a cedar. The sinews of its thighs are*
> *tightly knit together. Its bones are tubes of bronze.*
> *Its limbs are bars of iron. It is a prime example*
> *of God's amazing handiwork.*
> *Job 40:16-19*

Our God is an infinitely imaginative creator, a master craftsman. He delights in amazing us and bringing glory to himself through the dazzling array of creatures he has made. The more we learn about the unique and cleverly designed creatures with which he populated Earth, the more we marvel at him!

Let's talk to God!

MY JOURNAL

I think it's awesome, God, that you made this Ice Age creature:

_____

_____

_____

_____

It's my favorite because:

_____

_____

_____

_____

MY PRAYER

God, your Ice Age creatures were marvels of design, able to withstand the cold and thrive in a chilly world. I want to spend some time today praising you for being my amazing Creator. Where there was nothing, you made a beautiful universe. Where there was blackness, you made light. Where there was emptiness, you designed amazing plants and creatures. How awesome you are, my Creator!

A mammoth tooth was made for chewing tough veggies. This one is just a little longer than a shoe box.

Do you like circuses? The shows under the big top are famous for their wild and exotic animals. If you lived in the Ice Age, every day would be a circus! The cool creatures on parade were even weirder than those at Ringling Bros. and Barnum & Bailey. There were ancient camels and striped zebrine horses, and lion tamers would have had a challenge with those saber-toothed cats.

What would the circus be without elephants? The Ice Age had its own version—mammoths! Spectacular, furry versions of today's Dumbos, they stood over thirteen feet high at the shoulder. (It's big. It's huge! It's, well, mammoth!) Mammoths had four teeth the size of backpacks, two on top and two on the bottom. They used them to chew up seven hundred pounds of veggies every day. Mammoths used their trunks the way elephants do, pulling up plants to eat. Their tusks were fourteen feet long.

Ice Age animals have not been gone long enough to have become fossilized as dinosaurs have. So we can learn about Ice Age creatures from their bones or their frozen remains. A frozen baby woolly mammoth was found in Siberia in 1977. His stomach still had buttercups in it from his last meal! In 1997 a nine-year-old boy who was herding reindeer found an even fresher mammoth frozen into the Siberian ground. The mammoth had been frozen since the last Ice Age, and scientists knew the only way to keep it "fresh" while they studied it was to keep it frozen. They carved out a thirty-three-ton cube of frozen earth around the mammoth.

Then a giant helicopter flew the oversized ice cube, with the mammoth's tusks sticking out of the side, to a cave where it could be studied and kept frozen. A mammoth's age can be determined by counting the rings inside its tusks, much like counting tree rings. This mammoth was forty-seven years old when it died.

Mammoths were strong and fierce when attacked. Hunters who lived in the Ice Age had to work in large groups when they went after these mega-elephants. Spear points and human bones have been found with mammoths, showing us that some hunters lost their lives while trying to bring down these massive animals. But it was worth the risk—a mammoth could feed many families for weeks. Since people didn't have refrigerators, they probably made lots of mammoth jerky!

Most risks today are not life-and-death, but they feel as real. When we are with non-Christian friends or relatives, we may *think* about sharing the gospel with them. But to actually *do* it feels about as risky as facing down a woolly mammoth! We come up with a million excuses not to share our faith. But we can find the courage and boldness to share the Good News by thinking, "This isn't a woolly mammoth—this is my friend! I'm not going to get trampled to death for telling how much Jesus has done for me." We can be sure that if we speak patiently and gently about our great God, it will please him. We can be God's tool to bring friends into a friendship with the Creator of the universe. That is worth a little risk!

Think about what God says to you

I live in eager expectation and hope that I will never do anything that causes me shame, but that I will always be bold for Christ . . . and that my life will always honor Christ, whether I live or I die.

Philippians 1:20

The apostle Paul wrote these words when he was in prison in Rome, waiting to see if he would live or die. His "crime" was sharing the gospel of Jesus Christ. But he wasn't afraid, because God was with him. Paul knew that God wanted him to tell others about Jesus, no matter what the consequences.

Let's talk to God!

MY JOURNAL

God, this is a friend who doesn't know you:

_____

This is what I might say to my friend:

_____

_____

_____

_____

MY PRAYER

Lord, give me opportunities to tell my friends about you. Give me the courage I need to talk about you. Give me gentleness and wisdom when I speak about you. Give me patience and understanding for those who do not believe, because you love them as much as you love me! Above all, help me to keep in mind that it is you, not me, who changes people's hearts to believe in you.

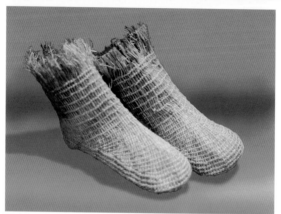

These grass stockings are similar to the ones Otzi wore inside of his deerskin boots. (Courtesy University of Alaska at Fairbanks)

On a warm day in the fall of 1991, two hikers walked along the edge of a glacier in Italy. Helmut and Erika Simon spotted what they thought was the head of a doll sticking out of the hard ice. When they took a closer look, they realized they were looking at the head and shoulders of a frozen person. They called the police, but when an Austrian scientist came, everyone realized that the Simons had discovered an Ice Age treasure—the mummy of a man who had taken his last hike a few thousand years ago.

This ice man was named Otzi (UTT-zee) after a nearby valley. But where did he come from? Where was he going? What was life like when he was hangin' around those mammoths and musk ox? Scientists found many clues as they studied the dried-out mystery man. Otzi had with him a stone knife with a wooden handle, an ax, and a big bow with some arrows. The best guess is that he was on a hunting expedition.

Ice Age people used stone tools, but Otzi's ax was a wonderful tool and weapon, with a blade made of metal. The blade was fastened to a wooden handle with cowhide and glue made from birch trees. At first, scientists guessed that the ax blade was

Otzi used tools similar to this ax and hammer, made by Stone-Age Inuit peoples of northern Alaska. Otzi's ax had a copper head.

bronze, which was used for tools about four thousand years ago. But to their surprise, the blade was copper, a much older metal. It turns out that the ice man was alive at least five thousand years ago, in the Copper Age!

Copper Age villages have been found near the place where Otzi's body was found. Otzi probably lived in a mud and wood house in one of those villages. Perhaps, like many houses of that time, it was built on stilts over a lake. Otzi wore a soft deerskin shirt and pants and leather shoes stuffed with grass to keep his feet warm. He had a container made of birch bark to carry things in, and he wore a leather necklace with a white stone disk hanging from it. His head was covered by a fur cap, and over his shoulders he wore a cape made from dried grass. He also carried dried antelope meat and berries, along with a kind of mushroom that is used for medicine.

Whatever happened to Otzi, this cool customer was well prepared for an Ice Age hunt. He probably went out one day planning to hunt for food and then return to his village. But he never got back.

God wants us to make plans, but we need to remember that he holds our future in his hands. He holds our very lives in his hands. He has the power and the right to change our plans. He knows the very day, hour, and minute when we will leave our earthly bodies and join him in heaven.

Think about what God says to you

Look here, you people who say, "Today or tomorrow we are going to a certain town and will stay there a year. We will do business there and make a profit." How do you know what will happen tomorrow? For your life is like the morning fog— it's here a little while, then it's gone. What you ought to say is, "If the Lord wants us to, we will live and do this or that."

James 4:13-15

God can certainly surprise us. Sometimes the surprises are welcome, sometimes they are not. But God has the right to step in and change our plans at any time. After all, he is the ruler of our lives!

Let's talk to God!

MY JOURNAL (choose one)

Lord, this is a time when you stepped in and changed my plans, and things turned out a lot better than they would have:

_____

_____

_____

_____

Lord, this is a plan I have that I need to let you step in and change if it's not what you want for me:

_____

_____

_____

_____

MY PRAYER

My life is yours, God. I know that, but sometimes I forget that my plans are yours too. Help me to grow into a person who is okay with any change you make in the plans I have.

Experiment: Cool Times in the Ice Age

Ice Age mammals had extra layers of fat to keep them warm. We can experience what these layers did to insulate them by using water and Crisco!

YOU WILL NEED:
- a kitchen or bathroom sink or a plastic bucket
- cold water, with one tray of ice cubes in it
- Crisco, lard, butter, or margarine

WHAT TO DO:
Fill your sink or bucket with cold water and ice cubes. This is what the weather was like in the Ice Age! Now, cover one hand with Crisco or margarine. Put both hands in the cold water, and leave them in for five seconds. Now take them out. Which hand feels the warmest? Which hand feels the coldest?

The Crisco acts like the fat layer of a woolly mammoth or musk ox. It keeps the cold out!

ILLUSIONS

Who has ever seen or heard of anything as strange as this?

Isaiah 66:8

Have you ever seen a full moon just when it's rising over the roofs or treetops in your neighborhood? It looks gigantic! But just wait. In an hour or so, it will climb higher into the sky, and it will look much smaller. You have witnessed the "moon illusion."

People often claim that the earth's atmosphere magnifies the moon. While the air causes the moon's shape to warp and wiggle, it doesn't become any larger at the horizon than it is when it's higher in the sky. So what's up? The moon seems to change size because of what our brain *thinks* it sees, not because of what it really does see. The moon illusion is a psychological effect—it's all in your head, dude! Scientists are not sure, but they believe that our mind compares the moon to objects near it, like a tree or a house, and concludes that the moon is gigantic. But as the moon goes up into the sky and we have no other objects next to it, our senses tell us that it is smaller. Check it out some night. (For a visual demonstration of this effect, see the "Three Girls" illusion in this week's painting on the previous page. It is explained in the Activity Ideas for Week 5.)

There are many illusions in the world. Some play tricks on our eyes. Some play tricks on our ears. But all of them can make us think something is true when it's not.

Jesus warned us about illusions in the spiritual realm. In Matthew 23:27-28, he talked to the Pharisees about how they tried to create the illusion that they were godly men: "You are like whitewashed tombs—beautiful on the outside but filled on the inside with dead people's bones and all sorts of impurity. You try to look like upright people outwardly, but inside your hearts are filled with hypocrisy."

On the Mount of Olives, Jesus warned his followers about another illusion—false messiahs. "If anyone tells you, 'Look, here is the Messiah,' or 'There he is,' don't pay any attention. For false messiahs and false prophets will rise up and perform great miraculous signs and wonders so as to deceive" (Matthew 24:23-24).

Think about what God says to you

> They see what I do, but they don't perceive its meaning.
> They hear my words, but they don't understand.
>
> Mark 4:12

There will always be Pharisees and false messiahs running around, just as there were at the time of Christ. Today we have to deal with modern-day illusions about the Christian life.

Let's talk to God!

MY JOURNAL (choose one)
Here are three typical illusions about what it means to be a Christian. Pick the one you're most interested in, then look up the "Illusion Buster" verse below it, and write out the truth in your own words!

Illusion 1: *Because I'm a Christian, God will protect me from pain and suffering.*

Illusion Buster: I Peter 4:12-19

God, I wish I'd never have to suffer, but I probably will. I must trust you to be with me because your Word says:

_____

_____

Illusion 2: A Christian shouldn't feel angry, sad, or depressed.
Illusion Buster: Psalm 34:18

Lord, sometimes I do feel angry, sad, or depressed. When that happens, help me remember that your Word says:

_____

_____

Illusion 3: If bad things happen to me, it must be punishment from God because I sinned.
Illusion Buster: Psalm 34:19

Father in heaven, when troubles come, help me to remember that:

_____

_____

MY PRAYER

Dear Lord, there is so much to learn about life as a Christian. Please put people in my life who are wise and know you very well. That way I can learn from them what my life in Christ can be like, free from illusions and confusion, and rooted in your truth.

Proving the Moon Illusion

There is an easy way to show that the moon is the same size when it is low in the sky as it is when it is higher. Take a photo of the moon when it is close to the rooftops in your neighborhood. Wait for at least one hour and take another photo. When you get your pictures back, measure the moon. You will see that even though it *looks* like its size changes, the moon in each of your pictures will be the same size.

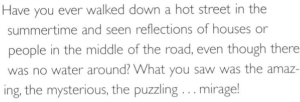

Have you ever walked down a hot street in the summertime and seen reflections of houses or people in the middle of the road, even though there was no water around? What you saw was the amazing, the mysterious, the puzzling . . . mirage!

Mirage (muh-*raj*) is a French word meaning "to look at." And just look at this: A perfectly dry street seems to have a puddle reflecting the things beyond it. How can this be? This wacky optical illusion is caused by bending light. Yep, light bends! Cool air is denser than warm air. When air is dense, light bends less than it does through thinner, hotter air. For a mirage to occur, the air needs to be very hot near the ground and cooler above. So, for example, the light from a palm tree behind the hot air is bent. Light from the bottom of the tree bends upward through the hot air, but light near the top of the tree passes through cooler air, so it doesn't bend much at all. Through the mirage, we see the real tree above and an inverted (upside-down) image of the tree below. The upside-down image looks just like the reflection in a pool of water!

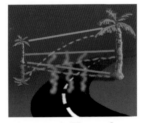

A mirage does a vanishing act when you get close to it. The reflection on the ground keeps moving away from you. This is because the mirage is simply bent light and is not attached to the ground. It isn't real.

You've heard people say, "Don't believe everything you see." Others may say, "Seeing is believing." Our senses can be fooled. Is that a pool of water, or just a hot sidewalk? When we get up to what seemed to be a pond, we see only asphalt. The reflection was only a faint and fleeting image of the real thing beyond.

Paul speaks of God in just this way. He knew that in this world we see the things of God only as a dim reflection, like looking into a "poor mirror." But one day we will see God face-to-face, and we will understand the things that in this world seemed to be bent reflections.

Think about what God says to you

> *Now we see things imperfectly as in a poor mirror, but then we will see everything with perfect clarity. All that I know now is partial and incomplete, but then I will know everything completely, just as God knows me now.*
>
> *1 Corinthians 13:12*

We don't understand everything now, but that's okay. Someday we will see God face-to-face, and the things that looked like wavering mirages will become clear to us. Our world is like a reflection. God is reality!

Let's talk to God!

MY JOURNAL (choose one)

Can I know you completely, God, while I'm here on earth? According to 1 Corinthians 2:9 and 2:16 I can't because:

_____

_____

_____

_____

Lord, this is something I really look forward to knowing about you when I get to heaven:

_____

_____

_____

_____

MY PRAYER

Lord, there are things that I see but don't understand. It is hard to understand the things of heaven when I'm living on this earth. Give me patience to understand things the way you would have me understand them. I look forward to the day when I can see your beautiful face and experience your love for me full force!

Have you ever wondered why the sound of the whistle seems to change pitch as a train travels by? The train whistle gets higher and higher as the train approaches, then gets lower and lower as the train moves away from you. If you asked him, the train engineer would tell you that the pitch of the whistle stays the same all the time. But you know better! The illusion that the pitch of a sound is changing is called the *Doppler effect*.

To understand the Doppler effect, you need to understand a little about how your ears work. Your ears are yet another amazing creation from God. Each ear has a tightly stretched flap of skin called an eardrum. It senses vibrations in the air. These vibrations are fed into your brain, where you experience them as sound. Sound is just vibrating air. The vibration of the air comes in waves toward you. If the sound waves are close together or have a high frequency, they sound high-pitched. But if the waves are farther apart or have a low frequency, the sound is low-pitched.

So let's get back to that train. As the train moves toward you, the sound waves get compressed toward you until they are very close together. So the noise of the whistle sounds high to your ears. As the train moves away from you, the sound waves shift in frequency. They get stretched farther apart by the retreating train, and the sound of the whistle is much lower to your ears. For you to experience the

Doppler effect, the object making the noise has to be in motion toward you or away from you. If you are on the train, there won't be that shift in the frequency of the sound waves, so the pitch of the whistle will stay the same.

Did you know that there are spiritual Doppler effects? They are called rumors. You can't believe everything you hear. And you sure don't want to pass on something you've heard without first finding out if it's true. Proverbs 14:15 says, "Only simpletons believe everything they are told! The prudent carefully consider their steps." How do you figure out if something you've heard is really true? Ask someone who is likely to know—maybe your mom, your dad, or a teacher.

Think about what God says to you

*Commit yourself to instruction; attune your ears
to hear words of knowledge.*
Proverbs 23:12

Rumors can scare and upset people. That's why Satan loves to use them for his purposes. Next time you hear a rumor, check it out. Then think carefully about whether this is something you should share with your friends. It pleases God a lot when you seek out the truth.

Let's talk to God!

MY JOURNAL (choose one)

Lord, I'm sorry I shared this rumor with a friend because later I found out it wasn't true at all:

_____

_____

_____

_____

_____

God, I know you are glad when I stop a rumor because:

_____

_____

_____

_____

MY PRAYER

Lord, I want to make you happy by checking out the facts before I share something that could upset or worry others.

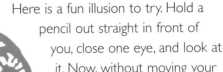

Here is a fun illusion to try. Hold a pencil out straight in front of you, close one eye, and look at it. Now, without moving your head, open your eye and close the other one. See how the pencil seems to move? What's up with that?

Your eyes are spaced about an inch apart, and each eye sees a slightly different, overlapping scene. That is why the pencil seems to jump when you change eyes. *Stereopsis* is the science-speak for what's happening here. It's also called binocular vision, and it's why 3-D movies and "Magic Eye" pictures work.

Did you know that your eye is designed like a camera? It has a pupil—the black thing in the middle of your iris—that adjusts for the light level by opening and closing. Behind that is a lens that focuses the image you are looking at. At the back of the eyeball, where a camera has film, is the retina, where the "picture" forms and is sent along the optic nerve to your brain.

Our eyes each see a flat picture of the world, like a photograph—just width and height. But when these two flat images combine, a miraculous thing happens: We can see the third dimension, depth! Our brains are wired to take the pictures from both eyes and show us a 3-D world. That means we can tell a lot more about shapes and distances than if we just had information from two dimensions.

The most powerful tool for judging distances is stereopsis. But what about people who only have one eye? How can they judge distances? Glad you asked. Fortunately, God has provided people with other cues for figuring out how near or far away an object is. We judge the distance of things in several ways. If we know how big something is, like a person, we can tell how far away it is by its size. If something is in front of something else, we know it is closer. We also judge distance by perspective. One example of perspective is when we look at train tracks. The parallel lines seem to get closer and closer until they touch at the horizon.

It takes these three things working together to give us a three-dimensional look at the world: two eyes and one brain. Did you know that God is three in one? He is God the Father, God the Son, and God the Holy Spirit. Like our two eyes and one brain, these three persons of God work together in our lives to give us good spiritual vision, depth perception, and perspective.

Think about what God says to you

Jesus came and told his disciples, . . . "Therefore, go and make disciples of all the nations, baptizing them in the name of the Father and the Son and the Holy Spirit."
Matthew 28:18-19

This is a very helpful verse for understanding that God is three persons in one. Jesus says, "In the name of the Father and the Son and the Holy Spirit." He doesn't say "names." He says "name," which shows us that he is talking about one Person.

Let's talk to God!

MY JOURNAL (choose one, two, or all three)

God the Father, another name for you is "Jehovah mighty in battle"
(Psalm 24:8, ASB). Knowing this helps me see that:

_____

_____

_____

_____

God the Son, another name for you is "Servant" (Philippians 2:7, NIV).
Knowing this helps me see that:

_____

_____

_____

_____

God the Holy Spirit, another name for you is "Counselor—the Spirit of
Truth" (John 15:26). Knowing this helps me see that:

_____

_____

_____

_____

MY PRAYER

Dear God, thank you for being Three-in-One. Thank you for being "Jehovah
mighty in battle." I don't have to fear anything with you in my life. Any
battle I have to fight has already been won by you. Thank you for being
Jesus, the "Servant." You came to earth to save me and show me how to
humbly serve others. Thank you for being the Holy Spirit, the
"Counselor—the Spirit of Truth." Your truth will protect me from Satan's
illusions and lies.

The greatest illusion of all is when people claim they can see into the future. Since the dawn of history, humans have tried to predict what will happen. The ancient Greeks set up *oracles*—priests or priestesses who went into trances to discover the future. Once in a while they guessed right.

Perhaps the most famous predictor of future events was Nostradamus, an astrologer, physician, and poet who lived in France in the 1500s. His poems about the future used a lot of symbols, and many have claimed that they accurately predicted world wars, assassinations, and other famous events. But most of the predictions were so symbolic that people can interpret them in different ways. The clear ones have been wrong. Nostradamus wrote a horoscope for the son of a famous French judge, and not one prediction came true!

A popular way of predicting the future these days is astrology. We can read our horoscope in almost any newspaper, but astrology actually started out as a religion in ancient Mesopotamia. Astrology says that the position of the stars and planets when we are born affects our lives.

There are many problems with astrology. Back in A.D. 400, the church leader Augustine realized that astrology didn't work when he learned that a rich man and his slave were born on the same day and should have had the same fate! Astrology claims to be a valid science, but it's based on the belief that there are six planets and that the sun is not the center of our solar system.

The Bible says God is in control of our fate, not the stars. God tells us, "Do not act like other nations who try to read their future in the stars. Do not be afraid of their predictions, even though other nations are terrified by them. Their ways are futile and foolish" (Jeremiah 10:1-3). The Bible also says that a true prophet must be correct every time. Nostradamus, oracles, and horoscopes don't come close. Prophecy in the Bible is 100 percent true 100 percent of the time!

There are 321 predictions about the coming of Christ, most made several hundred years before Jesus came. Here is one of them: "He had done no wrong, and he never deceived anyone. But he was buried like a criminal; he was put in a rich man's grave" (Isaiah 53:9). This prophecy of Isaiah was written over seven hundred years before Jesus was crucified and buried in a rich man's grave, a stone tomb belonging to Joseph of Arimathea. God gave people a specific prophecy so that they would recognize Jesus when he came as God's Son and their Savior.

Think about what God says to you

I am the Lord. . . . Everything I prophesied has come true, and now I will prophesy again. I will tell you the future before it happens.
Isaiah 42:8-9

Our God knows the beginning and the end, and he gave people clues in the Old Testament so that they would know when his Son came to Earth. God knows our future too, and he is lovingly bringing it about.

Let's talk to God!

MY JOURNAL (choose one)

This is one thing I have heard about the future, Lord, that is probably not true:

_____

_____

_____

_____

This is why I think only you can tell us the truth about the future, God:

_____

_____

_____

_____

MY PRAYER

Lord, thank you that I can trust you for my future. When life is confusing or when I hear predictions that are not based on your Word, I know that I can trust your Word to be true.

Address This!

Biblical prophecy is like an address on an envelope. Some predictions are like the bottom line: they're general enough only to show us the city, state, or country. But some are more specific, like the street address. And some are as specific as the name at the top of the address.

For instance:

Frank Jones (the Messiah)
6280 W. Chestnut Ave. (buried in a rich man's tomb)
Littleton, Colorado 80128 (born in Bethlehem)

Now see if you can put these prophecies about Jesus in order, the most general one at the bottom, then more specific, then the most specific one on the top line:

• will be a descendant of King David (Jeremiah 23:5)
• will be sold for thirty pieces of silver (Zechariah 11:12)
• will be called Immanuel—God with us (Isaiah 7:14)

1. _____
2. _____
3. _____

Stereo Activity for Day 4

Can you see in 3-D?

Put your book flat on a table. Now take a small mirror and hold it vertically like a wall between the two images, with the mirror facing left. Put the edge of the mirror against your nose, and keep your face about half a foot above the book. With your right eye, look at the picture on

the right. With your left eye, look at the reflection of the left picture that you see in the mirror. (See diagram.) Move the mirror around a little until the two pictures line up. *Wow!* Suddenly, you will see that trees are in front of buildings and the bird is floating in the sky!

Illusions: The Week 5 Painting

Turn back to the beginning of this week to the "bizarro" painting of a train. The train represents shifting sounds.

1. What is this sound effect called?
2. How many faces do you see in the picture, counting the three girls? (Hint: Do you see vases or faces?)
3. The symbols in the sky are astrological symbols. What is astrology? Can you remember a reason that astrology is not true?
4. Which of the three girls is the tallest? You may need a ruler to figure it out.

Answers are upside-down at the bottom of the page.

Answers

1. The shifting of sound (or light) is called the Doppler effect.
2. There are actually nine. The outsides of the vases form the outline of five faces. There is a face in the smoke to the far left, and three girls make nine!
3. Astrology is an ancient religion based on the position of the stars and planets in the sky—positions that have changed over time. It's based on the belief that there are only six planets. Also, if astrology were true, twins would lead identical lives, as would people born under the same sign of the zodiac, or stars.
4. The girls are all the same size. The background makes one look tall and another look small. This is what happens with the moon illusion.

ANIMALS
of the Bible

Ask the animals,
and they will teach you. . . .
Let the fish of the sea
speak to you. . . .
For the life of
every living thing
is in his hand, and the
breath of all humanity.

Job 12:7-8, 10

There are about twenty-five hundred different species of snakes in the world. Did you know that:

- only one-tenth of snake species are poisonous?
- snakes have no eyelids and cannot blink?
- an Asian python can swallow a deer whole?
- snakes are deaf—the only way they can "hear" sound is by sensing sound vibrations in the ground?
- snakes feel and smell with their tongues?
- the snake's stomach juices are so strong they can dissolve and digest bone?
- some snakes have over six hundred ribs?
- snakes' eggs are stretchable and get bigger as the baby snake grows inside them?

All the snakes mentioned in the Bible are poisonous. The Bible often uses the snake as a symbol of evil, trickery, danger, and death. The most common snake in Bible times was probably the carpet viper. There are still plenty of carpet vipers around today; they live all through the deserts and dusty hills of Palestine. The carpet viper has supertoxic venom and an especially aggressive temper. One drop of its venom is enough to kill several people. The snakes that bit the Israelites wandering in the desert were probably carpet vipers: "The people grew impatient along the way, and they began to murmur against God and Moses. 'Why have you brought us out of Egypt to die here in the wilderness?' they complained. 'There is nothing to eat here and nothing to drink. And we hate this wretched manna!' So the Lord sent poisonous snakes among them, and many of them were bitten and died" (Numbers 21:4-6). What the Bible doesn't say is that the venom of the carpet viper takes several days to kill a victim. As the venom destroys the blood cells and blood vessels, the victim slowly bleeds to death inside.

The Bible uses the snake as a symbol of what God hates. When we gossip about other people, we have a lot in common with the snake. Our poison tongues can do a lot of damage. The people we gossip about really suffer. Even if they act as if their feelings aren't hurt, they are bleeding on the inside. God hates it when we hurt others by gossiping.

Think about what God says to you

O Lord, rescue me from evil people. Preserve me from those who are violent, those who plot evil in their hearts and stir up trouble all day long. Their tongues sting like a snake; the poison of a viper drips from their lips.

Psalm 140:1-3

When you are tempted to gossip, remember the snake. Even a little poison is deadly. Even a drop is too much. When someone starts to gossip, you may feel tempted to join in, but *don't*. Take a stand. Here are a few things you can do:

1. Change the subject.
2. Say, "Let's not talk about her behind her back."
3. Leave the room.
4. Start an "Up Front" club with your friends. Agree together not to talk about people behind their backs.

Let's talk to God!

MY JOURNAL

Dear God, this is how I feel when people gossip about me:

_____

_____

_____

_____

This is how I feel after I gossip about someone else:

_____

_____

_____

_____

MY PRAYER

Dear Lord, the Bible shows me how much you hate gossip and how deadly gossip can be. I want to stop talking about others behind their backs and to help my friends stop too.

Snake Venom May Help Prevent Heart Attacks

One major cause of heart attacks is blood clots. A blood clot can break free from an artery and lodge in the heart, blocking the flow of blood and causing a heart attack. The venom of most vipers has special proteins that keep the blood platelets from sticking together, and this causes the victim to bleed to death internally. But a tiny bit of this venom is being used in a new drug that will be given to people who tend to get blood clots and are in danger of heart attacks. Way to go, scientists!

DAY 2: THE FISH

Have you ever wondered how a fish manages to breathe under water? Most fish don't have lungs. Instead, the fish uses its gills to breathe. Gills are wispy little curtains of body tissue inside a fish. The fish takes in water through its mouth, and the gills go to work, absorbing oxygen out of the water and passing it on to the bloodstream. Then the fish pushes the used water out through the gill slits in the side of its body.

For most New Testament villagers on the Sea of Galilee, fishing was a way of life. A hardworking fisherman could make a very good living. The fishermen usually worked at night. They used nets, either single-boat nets or bigger nets stretched between two boats working together. Some of the fishermen used a light to attract the fish, which were then speared. The Sea of Galilee is actually a big freshwater lake, and most of the fish caught were probably carp and tilapia. The carp is a bottom-feeding fish that can grow up to two or three feet long. The tilapia is a spiny-finned fish that incubates its eggs in its mouth. Mmmmm!

Fish were a great source of nutrition for the people of the Bible.

Fish were salted, pickled, or dried to preserve them to sell, to eat later, or to snack on while traveling away from home. Lunchtime? Just pull a dried fish out of your pocket and munch away. Yum!

Seven of Jesus' disciples were fishermen. He told them, "Come, be my disciples, and I will show you how to fish for people!"(Matthew 4:19). In the first century A.D. it was a good occupation to be a fisherman, but it was very dangerous to be a "fisher of people." It wasn't safe to talk openly about being a Christian, and worship was done in secret behind locked doors. So how did Christians find other Christians? They used the symbol of a fish as a secret code to represent their new life in Christ. They casually drew a picture of a fish in the dirt and watched to see if the other person responded. The Greek word for fish is $I\chi\Theta Y\Sigma$ (IK-thoos). These are the first letters of this code:

I=Jesus
χ=Christ
Θ=God's
Y=Son
Σ=Savior

Think about what God says to you

*God blesses those who are persecuted because
they live for God, for the Kingdom of Heaven is theirs.
God blesses you when you are mocked and persecuted and lied
about because you are my followers. Be happy about it! Be very
glad! For a great reward awaits you in heaven. And remember,
the ancient prophets were persecuted, too.*
Matthew 5:10-12

Did you know that today some Christians are still hated, hunted, thrown in jail, and killed? They have to worship God in secret. If they are "fishers of people," sharing the gospel with others, they risk their lives. It is a criminal offense to be a Christian in Sudan, China, Iran, and Iraq. The Christians in these countries need our prayers.

Let's talk to God!

MY JOURNAL (choose one)

I can remember one time, Lord, when I had to pay a price for following you:

_____

_____

_____

_____

Even if I would be ridiculed or in danger for worshiping you, God, it would be worth it to me because:

_____

_____

_____

_____

MY PRAYER

Lord, please protect the Christians in Sudan, China, Iran, and Iraq. Please keep them safe, and keep them from being lonely and discouraged. Fill them up with your Spirit and your peace, and help them to be brave.

Go Eat Some Fish!

God made fish one of the most nutritious sources of food on the planet. Fish have omega fatty acids in them, making them extra good for the human body. Studies have shown that eating fish gives people energy, helps keep body temperature normal, helps the body fight against illness, helps allergies get better, and even improves attention deficit disorder.

DAY 3: THE SHEEP

The sheep is an important Middle-Eastern animal and an important symbol in the Bible.

The first sheep were tamed 7,000 years ago. Sheep are mentioned about 750 times in the Bible, which shows how important they were to the people of that time.

Through the centuries sheep have been pretty handy for us humans to have around. They have been raised for use in religious sacrifices, for meat to eat, for milk and cheese, for sheepskin to wear or sleep on, and for wool that is spun into thread and woven into clothing. In Bible times, people didn't put money in banks like we do today. The wealth and security of many Israelite families was measured by the size of their flock of sheep. Their sheep were like woolly little bank accounts.

Sheep usually mate in the fall, and their lambs are born the following spring. At that time the shepherds stay out in the fields with the flock all night to help with the lambing and to keep away predators. Many Bible scholars think Jesus was born in the springtime based on the following verse: "And in the same region there were some shepherds staying out in the fields, and keeping watch over their flock by night" Luke 2:8 (NASB).

Sheep are stupid, defenseless, don't know what's best for them, and have an amazing ability to wander off and get themselves into trouble.

The Bible says many times that people are like sheep. Not a very flattering comparison! You can see why sheep need a shepherd. The shepherd talks and sings to his flock. Over a period of time, just as your dog or cat learns to recognize and respond to your voice, the sheep learn to respond to the shepherd's voice. They will not follow a stranger's voice.

Think about what God says to you

[Jesus said,] "He calls his own sheep by name and leads them out. After he has gathered his own flock, he walks ahead of them, and they follow him because they recognize his voice. They won't follow a stranger; they will run from him because they don't recognize his voice."

John 10:3-5

Just as the sheep know their shepherd's voice, we can learn to recognize Jesus' voice; but to do this, we need to spend time with him. Some of the ways we can spend time with Jesus include talking with him in prayer, reading the Bible, going to church and Sunday school, listening to Christian music, working on a daily devotional book, or being part of a Bible study group.

Let's talk to God!

MY JOURNAL

Lord, I don't want to get confused and follow the wrong shepherd. These are some things I want to do to learn to recognize your voice:

_____

_____

_____

_____

MY PRAYER

Dear Lord, there is so much peace and safety in knowing your voice. If I learn to recognize it and follow it, I won't be led astray. All I have to do is be willing to spend time with you, and I am willing. I will spend some time with you today and get to know you better.

Sheep Shenanigans

Q. What do you get when you cross a sheep with an elephant?
A. A woolly mammoth.

Q. Where does a sheep go to get a haircut?
A. To the baa-baa shop.

Q. What time is it when a dozen wolves are chasing a sheep?
A. Twelve after one.

Q. Why couldn't the sheep turn her car around?
A. The sign said no ewe turns permitted.

Q. What do little lambs love to do with their friends?
A. Have sheepovers.

Terrible Tongue Twister

The sixth sheik's sixth sheep's sick.

"The perfect killing machine." That pretty much describes the crocodile, which has been around since dinosaur times and shows no sign of leaving this earth any time soon. Like all reptiles, the crocodile is cold-blooded, spending as much time as possible basking in the sun for warmth and energy. It has a very slow metabolism and can go up to six months without eating. One of the largest carnivores on earth, the crocodile relies on camouflage, stealth, and infinite patience to catch its prey. It can go from looking like a floating piece of wood to becoming your worst nightmare as it chases you with lightning speed. Crocodiles swallow their prey whole unless it's too big, in which case they dismember it and swallow each piece whole. I guess the crocodile parents don't teach their young ones the importance of chewing their food and not gulping!

The Nile crocodile mentioned in the Bible can grow to be eighteen feet long. In fact, crocodiles, like the other members of the reptile family, never stop growing their whole lives! The Nile crocodile can weigh almost a ton and live up to seventy years. The crocodile has no fear of man or beast as it hunts along the river. It will attack and eat lions, tigers, and hippos. The Bible describes it like this: "The crocodile makes the water boil with its commotion. It churns the depths. . . . There is nothing else so fearless anywhere on earth. Of all the creatures, it is the proudest. It is the king of beasts" (Job. 41:31, 33-34).

The one creature the Nile crocodile will not eat is the Egyptian plover bird. This bird walks trustingly into the croc's open mouth and picks food from its fearsome teeth in perfect safety. I wonder which gutsy Egyptian plover first tried that little stunt. What was he thinking at the time? Maybe, "Hey, I've got an idea. Why don't I just walk into that crocodile's mouth and see if I can get a free lunch!" Anyway, whichever plover it was, I would like to shake his wing! That took a lot of bravery. It also took a lot of trust.

Have you ever felt like a little plover in the mouth of a crocodile? The truth is, we are completely helpless and powerless against many of the forces in our lives. But God is always with us. We can face evil and uncertainty because we have him beside us.

Think about what God says to you

The helpless put their trust in you.

Psalm 10:14

God is worthy of our trust 24/7. He is worthy of our trust every hour of every day—today, yesterday, and tomorrow. There will never be a time when we cannot trust him for everything we need.

Let's talk to God!

MY JOURNAL (choose one)

Sometimes, God, I feel really helpless when:

_____

_____

_____

_____

Lord, one time when I was helpless to change things, you did this for me:

_____

_____

_____

_____

MY PRAYER

Dear God, thank you. Thank you that I can trust you twenty-four hours a day, seven days a week, fifty-two weeks a year, for as long as I live. You protect the plover bird from the crocodile, and you protect me from evil that is stronger than a crocodile's teeth. I can rest and relax, knowing that you are watching over me.

God did an amazingly fantastic job when he created the lion. He created an animal that:

- has ears keen enough to hear prey a mile away
- has the largest eyes of any predator and can see perfectly in the dark
- has a roar that can be heard for four miles
- can run at the speed of forty miles per hour and jump four car lengths
- can leap tall buildings in a single bound (well, at least a one-story building)
- can take down prey three times its size
- can devour sixty pounds of meat in one meal
- can grow ten feet long from the tip of his nose to the tip of his tail and weigh up to five hundred pounds (males only—sorry, ladies!)

The strong, beautiful, bold, cunning Asian lion used to live through-out the Bible lands, but not anymore. Lion hunting was once the sport of kings; over the centuries the lion was hunted until it vanished from the Near East. In Bible times, Egyptian pharaohs took lions into battle with them as symbols of power and courage.

Although the Asian lion is gone from the Near East, we can learn a lot about lions and their behavior by studying the African lions living safely in wildlife preserves in Africa. All other wild cats live alone, but lions are sociable and live in big groups of ten to thirty lions. Each group is called a pride. Lions work together to hunt and care for the cubs. There's something interesting to notice when watching these big cats at rest. The fierce male lions are patient and gentle with the rowdy little cubs, who attempt to wrestle with them, bite at their tails, and never give them a moment's peace!

Gentleness is not weakness. No one could say a lion is weak! Gentleness is really power under control. The male lions curb their majestic power with the lion cubs. Jesus is gentle. But make no mistake, he is not weak. He is more powerful than all the lions in the world, and the gentleness he shows us is power under control.

Think about what God says to you
Both of the following verses refer to Christ:

He will be gentle—he will not shout or raise his voice in public. He will not crush those who are weak or quench the smallest hope.
Isaiah 42:2-3

Stop weeping! Look, the Lion of the tribe of Judah, the heir to David's throne, has conquered.
Revelation 5:5

These verses show us how powerful Christ is: "He will not crush those who are weak" tells us that Christ has the power to crush. "The Lion . . . has conquered" tells us he has defeated Satan. But the verse in Isaiah also shows us that Jesus is gentle, for he will *not* crush the weak.

Let's talk to God!

MY JOURNAL

This is a time when I was glad that Jesus was gentle with me, showing me his "power under control":

_____

_____

_____

_____

MY PRAYER

Dear God, I praise you and thank you that your Son, Jesus, has the power to destroy the whole world, but instead he came to earth in gentleness to save us.

Book Review

The Bible refers to Jesus as the "Lion of Judah." There is a great adventure/fantasy book by C. S. Lewis called *The Lion, the Witch and the Wardrobe*. It uses this image of Christ as a lion. If you haven't read it, go get it. Bet you'll love it!

Ridiculous Riddles

Q. What do you get if you cross a snake with a magician?
A. Abra da cobra.

Q. What's green and dangerous and good at math?
A. A crocodile with a calculator.

Q. What's the difference between a crocodile and a mailbox?
A. If you don't know, you'd better be really careful when you mail a letter.

Q. What do snakes study in school?
A. *Hiss*tory.

BOTANY
101

Then the Lord God planted a garden
in Eden, in the east, and there
he placed the man he had created.
And the Lord God planted all sorts
of trees in the garden—
beautiful trees that produced
delicious fruit. At the center
of the garden he placed the tree
of life and the tree of the
knowledge of good and evil.

Genesis 2:8-9

Look around you. Do you realize that most of what you see is made from plants? Some of the clothes you are wearing are probably made from cotton, and the colored dye is made from plants. The couch you are sitting on has a frame made from trees. The paint on the walls is made from latex, which comes from a plant. The paper pages of the book you are reading are made from trees. The gas in your car is a plant product! What else do you see that is made from plants?

When we study the plant world, God's creativity is crystal clear. For instance, did you know:

- there are tiny plants called *diatoms* that have only one cell?
- giant kelp can grow twelve inches a day?
- rose petals have special light-reflecting cells that attract insects?
- ferns, tulips, and strawberries reproduce without seeds?
- plants continue to grow bigger their whole lives?
- many plants have both male and female reproductive organs?
- there are fruits that explode to scatter their seeds?
- coconuts dropped by palm trees on the beach float to other islands to grow?

- birds and bats carry eaten seeds hundreds of miles before "dropping" them so they can grow?

God loves plants. They're an important part of his creation. But he loves us even more. There are many verses in the Bible that compare us to plants. Ezekiel 16:7 says, "I helped you to thrive like a plant in the field. You grew up and became a beautiful jewel." Six of the parables, or stories, that Jesus told to explain the Good News of salvation were about plants!

Think about what God says to you

Here is another story Jesus told: "The Kingdom of Heaven is like a farmer who planted good seed in his field. But that night as everyone slept, his enemy came and planted weeds among the wheat. When the crop began to grow and produce grain, the weeds also grew. The farmer's servants came and told him, 'Sir, the field where you planted that good seed is full of weeds!' 'An enemy has done it!' the farmer exclaimed. 'Shall we pull out the weeds?' they asked. He replied, 'No, you'll hurt the wheat if you do. Let both grow together until the harvest. Then I will tell the harvesters to sort out the weeds and burn them and to put the wheat in the barn.' "

Matthew 13:24-29

Here on planet Earth unbelievers live side by side with believers like the weeds mixed with the wheat in the story. Finally, on the judgment day, God will separate them out. That's why we need to be careful to tell our non-Christian friends about Jesus.

Let's talk to God!

MY JOURNAL

Jesus, this is why I think you used so many stories about plants when you taught the people:

_____

_____

_____

_____

MY PRAYER

Dear God, thank you for teaching me about yourself through the world of plants.

Match-up

Draw a line from the characters in the story of the weeds to what you think they represent. (If you get stuck, look up Matthew 13:36-43.)

the farmer	people who belong to Satan
the field	people who belong to Jesus
the good seed	angels
the enemy	Satan
the weeds	the world
the harvest	the end of the world
the harvesters	Jesus

DAY 2: THE ORIGINAL SOLAR POWER FACTORY

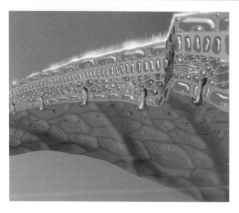

What is your favorite plant? A maple tree, an evergreen, a petunia, a jungle vine, a raspberry bush, a soft green lawn, or pond scum? All these plants give us fresh air to breathe by taking in carbon dioxide and putting out oxygen. They cover our world with a green blanket of life.

Each green plant has a substance called *chlorophyll,* which captures the energy of sunlight. No matter if it is a single-celled diatom or a towering redwood, a plant makes its own food by combining sunlight, water, and nutrients to produce sugar and oxygen. This amazing process is called *photosynthesis.* Each leaf on a plant is like a tiny factory. The raw materials of light, water, and nutrients are brought into the factory, and the finished product is shipped out: The sugar feeds the plant, and the oxygen by-product is released into the air for us to breathe.

The inner part of the leaf where all this happens is called the *mesophyll.* The cells of the mesophyll are very delicate. They are protected by a waxy, thick skin on the outer surface of the leaf that lets light in but keeps water from evaporating out. But for photosynthesis to occur, the cell must be able to breathe, so the mesophyll has a series of tiny doorways called *stomates.* The doors on the stomate openings are called guard cells. During the day, the mesophyll "factory" is in full swing, taking in sunlight, making sugar, and generally having a good time. So during the day, the guard cells fill with water. As they get full, they bend outward and the stomate's opening gets big. At night, when the "factory" goes to sleep, the guard cells release their water, and the stomates close.

Stomates and their guard cells protect what is most important inside the leaf—the sugars and the water. They are the guardians of the source of food and life for the plant. What is the most important thing inside of us? Our souls are the most precious part of us because they will live forever. God protects us with peace, his own spiritual version of guard cells. Peace means that his living water doesn't "evaporate" out of us when life becomes full of stress and craziness. Thank goodness for our spiritual guard cells, God's peace in our lives.

Think about what God says to you

> *His peace will guard your hearts and minds*
> *as you live in Christ Jesus.*
> *Philippians 4:7*

God's peace protects our hearts from drying up with worry, anger, bitterness, and resentment. His peace keeps us from feeling as if we should try to control everything that happens around us.

Let's talk to God!

MY JOURNAL (choose one)

Your peace, Lord, is able to guard my heart because:

_____

_____

_____

_____

MY PRAYER

Dear God, the world around me sometimes makes me worried. I get angry and frustrated by people and things, and this makes me feel like you are far away. But I know you are always close. I ask for your peace to guard my heart, keeping away fear and anger so that your powerful peace rules!

God's Peace

Draw a line from the words on the left to the correct words on the right.

angry
calm
content
dissatisfied
fighting
friendly
quiet heart
trusting
worried

I *have* peace.

I *need* peace.

DAY 3: Plants That Heal

Ancient people used all kinds of plants and many different parts of them to treat pain, sickness, and infections. The forests and meadows were their pharmacy. They learned by trial and error what worked and what didn't, and they learned how much of each plant to use. We still use many of these herbal cures today. There are healing elements in almost every part of different plants. If we listed all the healing plants that God has made, it would fill up this entire book; so instead we'll just list a few:

- The seed pods of the opium poppy are used to make morphine and codeine, which are strong painkillers.
- Willow bark was used long ago to lower fevers and stop pain and swelling; its modern cousin is aspirin.
- The roots of the Brazilian *Ipecacuanha* plant are used to make syrup of ipecac, which is used to get kids and pets to vomit after they've accidentally swallowed something poisonous. The leaves contain a drug that regulates the heartbeat.
- The bulbs, or cloves, of the garlic plant help cure colds and bronchitis. They also lower blood pressure and cholesterol.
- The red gum from the Australian bloodwood tree is used as an ointment to heal rashes, cuts, and sores. When watered down and used to gargle, it helps sore throats.
- The juice from the leaves of the aloe vera plant soothes burns.

God has given us hundreds of plants that can be used for healing. In many parts of the world natural herbs and extracts are still used every day to treat all kinds of wounds and sickness. In more techno-logically advanced countries, most of the medicines we use have been developed from plants. God has provided for us very well by giving us a plant kingdom with so many plants that can heal. He cares about our spiritual health and also about our physical health. He cares about all parts of us.

Think about what God says to you

> *On each side of the river grew a tree of life, bearing twelve crops of fruit, with a fresh crop each month. The leaves were used for medicine to heal the nations.*
> *Revelation 22:2*

Throughout the Bible, the tree is used as a symbol of life, of hope, and of God's goodness to us. The verse above describes the New Jerusalem after Jesus comes again. The tree mentioned here also represents the gift of eternal life, just like the tree of life in the Garden of Eden did. This verse says, too, that the leaves of this tree will someday be used to heal the spiritual sickness of the nations. That will be a happy day!

Let's talk to God!

MY JOURNAL (choose one)

Thanks, God, for this time when I used one of the medicines made from plants:

_____

_____

_____

_____

121

Lord, one time when I was "sick at heart" and you healed me was:

_____

_____

_____

_____

MY PRAYER

Dear God, thank you for being so creative and caring when you made the plant kingdom. You have provided me with plants that can heal my body. You sent your Son to heal my soul. Thank you for caring about all the different parts of me.

DAY 4: Plants That Feed Us

It wouldn't be possible for people to exist without plants. Up and down the food chain, plants provide all the food we eat: a grasshopper eats a leaf, then the grasshopper gets eaten by a chicken in the barnyard, which lays us some eggs for breakfast! Civilization began when people learned how to plant crops for food instead of just chasing their food around with spears! It must have been a happy day when the tired, wandering people could stop traveling and literally "put down roots."

A plant begins its life on the day the seed sprouts, or *germinates*. When a seed is put into the ground, it soaks up water and swells. This splits open the covering of the seed, or seed coat. If the embryo inside is alive and has started to grow, a root will come out of the seed to hold it firmly to the soil as it begins drawing in water and nutrients. Soon the shoot pushes out of the seed coat and out of the soil. The minute the sun hits it, the little plant begins photosynthesis.

A seed is just a seed. What makes the difference between a healthy plant and a sickly one is how the seed is planted and cared for as it grows. A wise and experienced farmer knows when to plant his seeds, how deeply and how far apart to plant them, how much water and fertilizer to give the plants, how to protect them from pests, and when to harvest the crop. The next time you say grace, why not thank God for the farmers who work long and hard to bring you the food you eat?

God created the seeds, but people have learned how to make them grow where and when they want them to. In the same way, God created the good news of the gospel, and one of our jobs here on earth is to spread the "seeds" of the gospel wherever and whenever God tells us to.

Think about what God says to you

> [Paul said,] "My job was to plant the seed in your hearts, and Apollos watered it, but it was God, not we, who made it grow."
> I Corinthians 3:6

The apostle Paul wrote this verse in his first letter to the Corinthians. He was a wonderful missionary, and Apollos was a gifted pastor. But in this verse, Paul reminds us that we need to be careful not to put our church leaders on the same level with God. They are only his servants. God is the one who saves people and helps them grow to become more and more like himself.

Let's talk to God!

MY JOURNAL

This week, Lord, I hope to plant the seeds of the gospel in this person's heart:

_____

_____

_____

_____

Help me, God, as I write my "action plan" for doing this. Here it is:

_____

_____

_____

_____

MY PRAYER

Dear God, thank you for giving me the job of spreading your Word. I will trust you to make the seeds I plant grow in the hearts of the people I talk to if it is your will.

DAY 5: Sci-Fi Plants

Thousands of years ago people first learned to plant seeds and grow their own food. People grew wheat and barley in the Middle East and Europe, rice in China, and corn in the Americas. If those ancient farmers saw the crops that modern farmers grow today, they wouldn't believe their eyes. Today crops grow twice as fast, they're twice as big, and they're bug resistant to boot! How is this possible? Farmers and scientists have worked together over the years to crossbreed the best plants and to develop chemical fertilizers and pesticides that will help the crops grow big and strong.

There is a downside to this, however. When we eat waxed, sprayed, chemically treated fruits and vegetables, we eat the chemicals, too. One way to avoid this is to scrub fruits and veggies very well before eating them. Another choice is to eat organic produce grown without chemical fertilizers and pesticides. Next time you are in the produce aisle, compare the organic produce to the regular produce. The organic fruits and veggies are much smaller and not as "pretty." They look a lot like the food our ancestors raised. They are also more expensive because they are harder to grow. But studies show that organic foods may have higher nutritional value than chemically raised produce. There are people who think we should ban chemical fertilizers and pesticides because they can hurt the environment and are not good for us. Other people point out that if we did this, food would cost three times as much, and there would be worldwide food shortages. What do you think about this?

Amazing breakthroughs are taking place in the world of farming.

Plants such as tomatoes and cucumbers, instead of being grown in soil, are grown in water with special minerals in it. This technique is called *hydroponics*. Genetically engineered plants provide large amounts of vitamins to help people in countries with poor nutrition.

Many people believe that we need to develop new "supercrops" to feed everyone. Others think that genetically engineered plants are a bad idea. They wonder what will happen if these supercrops mix with natural plants in the wild. Will it destroy the natural balance of plants?

Do the benefits of supercrops outweigh the dangers? It is a big challenge to balance all the factors. Part of growing up is learning that there are usually at least two points of view to every situation! God calls us to have balance in our lives too—not to lean too much in one direction or the other. This takes a lot of wisdom.

Think about what God says to you

> The chief official brought all the young men to King Nebuchadnezzar. The king talked with each of them, and none of them impressed him as much as Daniel, Hananiah, Mishael, and Azariah. . . . In all matters requiring wisdom and balanced judgment, the king found the advice of these young men to be ten times better than that of all the magicians and enchanters in his entire kingdom.
>
> Daniel 1:18-20

You probably do not have to make decisions about a kingdom, but you do make decisions about your life. God is pleased when you talk to wise people and make good, balanced decisions.

Let's talk to God!

MY JOURNAL

When the Bible doesn't say anything about a situation, this is how I figure out what I should do:

_____

_____

_____

_____

MY PRAYER

Dear Lord, sometimes I get so confused about all the opinions I hear about different things. I want to use your wisdom to balance out all the facts and opinions and come to a decision that honors you. I love you very much.

Experiment: Germinate a Seed

FOR THIS ACTIVITY YOU WILL NEED:

- several beans or peas from garden seed packets
- a clear glass jar
- a paper towel
- an empty toilet-paper roll

1. Fold the paper towel so that it's short enough to fit inside the jar. Then line the inside of the jar with it.
2. Put the toilet-paper roll into the jar so it holds the paper towel against the sides of the glass. You may have to squish the roll a little to make it small enough to fit inside the paper towel.
3. With a pencil, poke the seeds down into the jar between the paper towel and the glass so you can see them. Space the seeds out so there is room between each of them.
4. Pour some water into the jar. Be sure to get the paper towel nice and wet. Leave about a half inch of water in the jar, just so it touches the paper towel to keep it moist.
5. Put the jar in a dark closet for a few days. Check to be sure the paper towel is staying damp. You can add water if needed.
6. When the seeds sprout, plant them in a pot and put it in a sunny window.

Draw a line to the word that finishes each sentence about the experiment. (If you get stuck, look back at Day 4.)

The dark closet represents the

● germinate

The part of the seed that grows upward is the

● root

Another word for sprout is

● shoot

The part of the seed that grows downward is the

● soil

Design a Make-Believe Flowering Plant

Get some colored pencils and design the leaves, the stem, the color, and the shape of the flowers of your plant. Does this plant bear fruit? If so, draw some of the fruit. Is any part of the plant good for making medicine? If so, write about that. Now come up with a name for this new plant!

THE MAMMALS

You care for people and
animals alike, O Lord.

Psalm 36:6

Friendships are important, even in the animal world. Monkeys, for instance, are very friendly and social. Mother rhesus monkeys do something interesting with their babies. When they see another baby monkey roaming free, they often go and pick it up, holding it and their own baby together in their arms for some time. They usually pick up babies whose moms have a higher social standing in the group! Scientists think the mothers are trying to start friendships between the two babies.

Just as with people, friendships between animals create a feeling of security, and companionship lowers their stress levels. Here's a good example from the primate world: Long-tailed macaques were confined alone in cages at a laboratory for some scientific research. Their keepers got concerned because the monkeys seemed very stressed and began biting themselves. So they put two monkeys in each cage—females with females, males with males (so they wouldn't end up with a zillion long-tailed macaques)! The monkeys stopped biting themselves and seemed much happier.

Grooming behavior is also a very important way for monkeys to feel secure. They spend lots of the day grooming each other. Humans don't spend hours going through a friend's hair, looking for fleas and lice! But we do show friendship by touching. A hug can help a friend who is having a bad day. A pat on the back gives encouragement. That's all a part of friendship.

A friend can teach us how to do something new. Imo, a young

Japanese macaque, is one very smart monkey. She figured out how to wash the sand off wheat before eating it. First she tossed the sandy wheat into some water. After the sand sank, she skimmed up the clean grains of wheat. Now all the monkeys in her troop have learned this new skill.

Friendships bring a lot of joy into our lives. But sometimes our friends disappoint us, and our friendships break up. That can really hurt. But if we turn to Jesus, the only Friend who won't ever let us down, he will give us comfort and encouragement during the lonely times. Jesus, our perfect Friend, doesn't want us to stop trying to have friendships here on Earth, though. Friends are part of God's plan for teaching us, for helping us grow, and for giving us fun times and happy memories. So never give up on friendship. It is worth the hard work.

Think about what God says to you

> *A friend is always loyal, and a brother is born to help in time of need.*
> Proverbs 17:17

God's idea of a good friend is someone who is true, faithful, and dependable. It is someone who is willing to help meet your needs. God gave King David a special friend like that. His name was Jonathan. God also gave Jesus and the disciples to each other. And he has given you and your friends to each other.

Let's talk to God!

MY JOURNAL (choose one)
Pick one of the following verses from Proverbs and tell God how you would like to be this kind of a friend.
Proverbs 27:9—Lord, this is the "heartfelt counsel" I want to give a friend.

Please make it "as sweet as perfume and incense":

_____

_____

_____

_____

Proverbs 27:10—This is a time when I need your help, God, to "never abandon a friend":

_____

_____

_____

_____

MY PRAYER

Dear Lord, thank you for giving me Jesus as my perfect Friend. Thank you for giving me friends here on Earth, too. I need your help so that I don't expect them to be perfect, and I need your grace to forgive them when they hurt my feelings. I want to spend more time thinking about how I can be a good friend and less time wishing my friends were better friends to me.

The mongoose is a small mammal native to southern Asia, Africa, and Spain. It looks a lot like a weasel and is about the same size. It sports a pointed face and a bushy tail. It is very adaptable, able to survive and thrive just about anywhere with a warm climate. Also, the mongoose is *definitely* not a picky eater! Mice, rats, lizards, insects, snakes, eggs, and fruit are all favorites.

The mongoose may be small, but boy, is it feisty! It is famous for its ability to kill a king cobra. Anyone who's read *Rikki-Tikki-Tavi* by Rudyard Kipling will never forget the courageous little mongoose who fought and killed two cobras, saving the lives of the humans he lived with. Ancient Egyptians domesticated the mongoose and considered it sacred. The mongoose was called "Pharaoh's Mouse" because it kept down the crocodile population of the Nile River by eating the crocodile's eggs. It also kept the rat and mouse population down nicely.

How does a mongoose manage to defeat a deadly cobra? By knowing its enemy and using the right tactics. When the mongoose and cobra face off, the mongoose's thick bushy hair stands on end; this helps protect it from the cobra's strikes. It darts around, getting the furious cobra to strike again and again as the mongoose dodges quickly. When the snake is exhausted, the mongoose grabs the snake's head in its jaws and crushes it. It then eats the snake's head and venom glands, which are not poisonous to a mongoose unless it's bitten. Although many young mongooses die fighting cobras, recent studies have shown that the mongoose can survive twenty times more venom than other animals the same size.

To defeat the enemy, you need to be brave and know his weaknesses. Do you know your enemy? He is Satan, the one "who leads the whole world astray" (Revelation 12:9, NIV). But remember, "the Spirit who lives in you is greater than the spirit who lives in the world" (1 John 4:4). "Resist the Devil, and he will flee from you" (James 4:7). And never forget that we've already won the battle! (See Revelation 20:7-10.)

Think about what God says to you

A final word: Be strong with the Lord's mighty power. Put on all of God's armor so that you will be able to stand firm against all strategies and tricks of the Devil.
Ephesians 6:10-11

Satan's goals spell his name. His goals are:

S: Suspicion—to make me suspicious of God's Word and God's faithfulness

A: All about me—to keep me at the center of my life instead of putting God there

T: Temptation—to tempt me to do the wrong thing

A: Attack—to attack my self-confidence

N: No fruit—to make sure I am able to do nothing good in the world

Let's talk to God!

MY JOURNAL (choose one)

This is one way Satan has attacked my self-confidence:

_____

_____

_____

And this is how I know you're going to help me defeat him, God:

_____

_____

_____

This is one way Satan has tried to make me suspicious of your faithfulness and truth, God:

_____

_____

_____

And this is how you're going to help me defeat him:

_____

_____

_____

MY PRAYER

Dear God, thank you for giving me the courage and the weapons I need to defeat Satan.

DAY 3: POLAR BEARS: MAGNIFICENT MOTHERS

A mother polar bear is really something special. Few mammals go through such hard work to raise their young. The pregnant polar bear relentlessly hunts seals until she has met her quota and gained the extra 440 pounds she will need to hibernate and to feed her cubs when they are born. (Ask your mom if she would be willing to gain 440 pounds for you!) Next, the polar bear mother-to-be must dig a snow or dirt den for herself and her expected cubs. In October she settles down in the den for the long winter hibernation. The cubs are usually born in January and are tiny and helpless. Most often two cubs are born, each weighing one or two pounds and measuring about twelve inches long. For the next three or four months the cubs spend their time nursing and cuddling up to their mother to keep warm. When spring arrives and their mother leads them out of the den, they weigh twenty to thirty pounds. The mother has dropped almost half her body weight from hibernation and nursing. Mother polar bear and her cubs hang around the den for a few weeks while she waits for them to get used to the cold temperature and to strengthen their legs for walking long distances. When she feels they are ready, the mother leads her cubs out onto the sea ice, stopping along the way to nurse them and let them rest. (Are we there yet, Mom?) When they reach the sea ice, she catches a nice, fat baby seal for them and gets them started on solid food.

There is danger as well as food out on the open ice. Male polar bears have been known to catch and eat polar bear cubs, which are tasty, fat little butterballs at this point. However, the mother bear will fight to the death to defend her young, so polar bear cubs don't get eaten too often.

The cubs learn how to hunt seals on land or sea by watching their mother. They stay with her for about three years until they are able to hunt on their own. Human children stay with their mothers a little longer than three years because there is so much more a human child has to learn to make it in this world. Your mom has a lot to teach you in the next few years. (If she can't do it, perhaps a grandmother, aunt, or big sister will.) She might teach you about responsibility, friendships, and building a life with God at the center—the most important teaching of all. Come to think of it, the polar bear has it easy!

Think about what God says to you

"Can a mother forget her nursing child?
Can she feel no love for a child she has borne? But even if that
were possible, I would not forget you!" [says the Lord.]
Isaiah 49:15

Both mothers and fathers can remind us of God's love for us, but each parent shows us that love in different ways. A mother's love is special because she is the one who "has borne" (or given birth to) her child. God says that his love for us is even greater than a mother's love.

Let's talk to God!

MY JOURNAL (choose one)

I remember one time, God, when my mom (grandma, aunt, sister) did something really special for me:

_____

_____

_____

_____

I think, Lord, that my mom has been a good mother in this way:

_____

_____

_____

_____

MY PRAYER

Dear God, thank you for giving me a mother (or someone else to take her place) who can watch over me and care for me. Thank you for telling me that you love me with that same strong love a mother feels for her child.

DAY 4: YOU PROBABLY HAVE A FOX FOR A NEIGHBOR!

Next time you're out at night in your neighborhood, keep your eyes peeled. If you see an animal running through the darkness across a lawn, look carefully. It might not be a dog or cat—it could very well be a fox! As their habitats have been destroyed by new construction, the clever foxes have learned how to survive in suburbia.

The fox is a member of the dog family. Foxes often live in groups, and they all help raise the cubs. A breeding pair will mate for life, which for a fox is about ten years. Foxes will eat anything and every-thing—insects, earthworms, squirrels, mice, birds, eggs, and roadkill. They especially love ripe fruit. Foxes are easily tamed when they're young and would make great pets except for one thing: They are nocturnal. As soon as its owners go to bed, the fox gets up and wants to play all night!

Foxes have been hunted and poisoned for centuries, but they are one of the most intelligent animals around and can figure out how to outsmart their human enemies. One hunter tells this story: He had spent all day boiling five fox traps in wood chips and water to get rid of the human scent. Then he set them in strategic places in the

141

woods, covering each one with leaves to disguise it. Finally, tired but proud of himself, he turned to go home, and there sat a fox. It had followed him all day and had soaked every trap site with its own scent to warn off other foxes!

Foxes can use their intelligence to learn complex new things. But more important than this is the fact that they are able to use this information for their benefit. We can't assume that we will grow and change just because we learn a lot about God and the Bible. Knowing about God isn't enough. Smart doesn't mean wise. Many people know a lot about God, but they aren't wise. They don't use their knowledge to change the way they think, talk, and act. Until we take what we've learned from the Bible and the Bible verses we've memorized and let these things change our hearts and lives, they're just useless bits of data. We need to put what we learn into action. That's true wisdom.

Think about what God says to you

> *The Lord in his kindness has given me wisdom that can be trusted, and I will share it with you.*
> *I Corinthians 7:25*

God is the giver of wisdom. He is willing to give if we are willing to receive.

Let's talk to God!

MY JOURNAL (choose one)

You can help me, God, to be smart and know things like:

_____

_____

_____

_____

You can help me, God, to be wise and do things like:

_____

_____

_____

_____

MY PRAYER

Dear Lord, you are the one who gives me the wisdom to make right choices. I know that wisdom isn't just about using my brain or showing how smart I am. It's also about using my heart. I want to understand what is good and what is fair, and I want to always choose the path that you have planned for me.

Horses have been tamed by humans for over four thousand years. But did you know that bands of wild mustangs still roam free in remote parts of our country? They don't need people to help them survive.

The story of how they got to America is fascinating. Christopher Columbus brought twenty horses with him on his second voyage to the New World. He started horse-breeding colonies in the Caribbean Islands. Soon many of the Caribbean horses were moved to the cattle ranches the Spaniards had set up in Mexico. Francisco Coronado took two hundred of these horses with him when he and his soldiers traveled north through Mexico to explore what is now the United States. Some of these horses wandered off or were stolen by Native Americans and then escaped. The wild stallions would often return to the ranches and lure off mares. Those stallions and mares are the ancestors of the wild mustangs of today. Small bands of them roam free in Nevada, Wyoming, Montana, and South Dakota. They are protected by federal law from being hunted and captured.

Not all wild horses live in the west. There are wild horses on Assateague Island in Virginia. Their ancestors probably swam to the island, escaping from a Spanish shipwreck. There are also wild horses in England, India, Tibet, Russia, and Australia.

Wild horses are beautiful, strong, and hardy—they have incredible endurance. If you ever get a chance to see a herd of these horses running free across the landscape, it will be an experience to remember forever.

The wild horse is a symbol of freedom. Another symbol of freedom is the cross. Jesus died on the cross to set us free from death, from fear, from guilt, and from sin. His death also allows us to be free from being controlled by our bodies, from living under a long list of rules, from worrying about what other people think about us, and from having conflict with God. In John 8:32, 36 Jesus said, "And you will know the truth, and the truth will set you free. . . . So if the Son sets you free, you will indeed be free."

Think about what God says to you

> *Christ has really set us free. Now make sure that you stay free, and don't get tied up again in slavery to the law.*
> *Galatians 5:1*

Freedom in Christ doesn't mean we're free to get our own way in everything. That just leads right back to sin. But we are free from guilt and fear, and from worrying about what other people think. The Pharisees had 630 laws that they added to God's commandments. The Jews struggled under this list of rules and regulations. But thanks to Jesus, we are free from those old rules, free to be fully alive as God created us to be. And we are free to serve Christ.

Let's talk to God!

MY JOURNAL

Choose one item from the list below that Jesus has freed you from:

- death
- sin
- fear
- conflict with God
- long lists of do's and don'ts
- being controlled by my body

The one I chose is important to me, Lord, because:

_____

_____

_____

_____

MY PRAYER

Dear God, I am learning your Word, and it is helping me to understand that I am really free from death, sin, guilt, and fear. Thank you that we don't have to live like the Pharisees, who had long lists of rules for everything. I want you to help me to stay free and to become the person you created me to be.

· ·

Wild Mustangs

If you would like to see wild mustangs, someday you might be able to go to the Bighorn Canyon National Recreation Area in Lovell, WY. This is on the border of southern Montana. At the visitor center they will give you directions to a likely viewing spot. The phone number is 307-548-2251.

· ·

ACTIVITY IDEAS FOR WEEK 8

Bearly Funny Jokes:

Q. Is it true that a polar bear won't attack you at night if you carry a flashlight?

A. It all depends on how *fast* you can carry the flashlight.

Q. What did the teacher call the nice, friendly, gentle, helpful polar bear cub?

A. A failure.

Q. What do little girl polar bears wear in their hair?

A. Bearettes.

Q. What do you get when you cross a polar bear with a kangaroo?

A. A white fur coat with a pocket.

Monkey Joke:

First monkey: Boy, do I have these scientists trained!

Second monkey: Really?

First monkey: Yeah. All I have to do is press this little buzzer, and one of them gives me something to eat.

Skunk Jokes:

Q. What do you get when you cross a bear with a skunk?

A. Winnie the Pooh.

Q. How do you keep a skunk from smelling?

A. Hold its nose.

147

Make a Mammal Habitat Diorama

Pick an animal you would like to design a habitat for. It can be one of those we talked about this week, a different mammal altogether, or you can make up your own animal the way you made up your own flower last week. Just use your imagination.

FOR THE HABITAT YOU WILL NEED:

- a shoe box
- construction paper
- glue
- tape
- scissors
- markers
- any of these you can find: small rocks, dry grass, pipe cleaners, green yarn

Put the shoe box on the table with the open end facing you so that the box has a top and sides. Now have fun cutting, pasting, coloring, and gluing the inside of the shoe box to create the habitat. Is it rocky? Is it snowy? Are there a lot of trees? Are there vines hanging down?

FOR THE MAMMAL YOU WILL NEED:

- construction paper or modeling clay to make the animal
- yarn
- carpet scraps
- craft fur or cotton balls to make the fur
- toothpicks
- pipe cleaners or straws to make the legs and the horns or antlers

After you are done making your mammal, put him or her in the habitat. You can glue or tape the animal to the back of the shoe box to help it stand up. If you have made up your own mammal, make a sign for the diorama that tells its name and some facts about it: a description of its habitat, its behavior, and what it eats.

DESERTS

I will make a pathway through the wilderness for my people to come home. I will create rivers for them in the desert! The wild animals in the fields will thank me, the jackals and ostriches, too, for giving them water in the wilderness.

Isaiah 43:19-20

It's hard to believe that the dry desert could blossom with life in the spring. (Photos courtesy Bill Gerrish.)

Just ask anyone who has flown on a space shuttle: Deserts are a *big* part of our little world. From orbit, looking down on Earth, tan and brown regions span the wide middle of Africa, then spread across Asia Minor, through northern India, and deep into China. In fact, desert and semidesert areas cover one-fourth of Earth's land.

Many famous deserts are mentioned in the Bible. Remember how the Israelites wandered in the desert for forty years after escaping from Egypt? They traveled through the Sinai and Negev (which means "dry" in Hebrew) deserts. There are other important deserts: To the east of the Nile River is the Arabian Desert, and to the west is the Sahara, the largest desert in the world. Close to the Nile, in the Sahara Desert, the great kingdoms of Egypt built huge pyramids and sphinxes.

The Bible speaks of the "Judean wilderness," where David hid from Saul. John the Baptist preached there, and it was probably where Jesus was tempted by Satan. The prophet Elijah went to the desert, where God kept company with him and sent ravens to feed him. Moses lived in the Midian Desert as a shepherd before he became the leader of God's people.

It's hard to believe that the desert could be anything but hot

and dry. Yet in the springtime, the world's deserts go through an amazing change. Each year for a few weeks, rain falls—big time. We're talkin' floods here. Flowers and plants burst out of the ground, casting their seeds to the wind for the next generation of desert plants. Grasses grow along the ravines and gullies. But it doesn't last long. The grasses that come up in the morning wither away by the hot afternoon.

What is one thing that God wants us to learn from the beautiful, brief blooming of the desert? "The hot sun rises and dries up the grass; the flower withers, and its beauty fades away. So also, wealthy people will fade away with all of their achievements" (James 1:11). God is interested in what lasts (our souls), not in what is temporary (our money and "stuff"). Like the grasses in the desert, the earthly things we do will all turn to dry dust. But the spiritual part of us will last forever because of our relationship with God and his Son, Jesus.

Think about what God says to you

Don't store up treasures here on earth, where they can be eaten by moths and get rusty, and where thieves break in and steal. Store your treasures in heaven, where they will never become moth-eaten or rusty and where they will be safe from thieves. Wherever your treasure is, there your heart and thoughts will also be.

Matthew 6:19-21

The things that seem so important to you today, like a new CD, the latest computer game, youth, beauty, wealth, and popularity, are not important to God. What is important to him is *you,* and he wants you to make him the most important thing in your life too!

Let's talk to God!

MY JOURNAL (choose one)

Here are some "earthly treasures" that I admit, God, are important to me:

_____

_____

_____

_____

Here is a way I want to store up treasures in heaven, Lord:

_____

_____

_____

_____

MY PRAYER

Lord in heaven, there are so many things in life that distract me and take me away from thinking about you. But even though they seem important now, I am on this earth for only a few years, and I will be with you forever. Help me to get my style straight and my stuff in order so that the things of earth are not as important to me as the things of heaven.

(Photo of a playa courtesy of Dr. Paula Messina.)

Just when you thought you knew what the desert was really like, here come the mysterious rock races of Death Valley, California! One area in Death Valley is called the Racetrack, because rocks seem to move around on the ground all by themselves. It's true, and it happens on the playas.

Playa is a Spanish word meaning "beach." A desert playa forms when a temporary desert river or downpour makes a pond. The pond dries into a level, hard basin. These desert flat spots are usually bright white from salt that has leached up from the ground and into the pond. If you get to a playa in the early morning, rocks that were in one place the night before have moved, leaving meandering trails behind them.

How could a stone move across the desert floor all by itself? Somehow, weather and geology work together to move these rocks. Scientists are still stumped, but they have some ideas. One guess is that when the playa gets wet, maybe from the scant dew in the desert night, it becomes slick. Rocks that have fallen onto the surface from the nearby hills and cliffs may be shuffled across the slippery playa by the evening wind. In the morning, the playa dries out almost instantly in the sun, leaving the shifting stones in new places. But that's just a guess.

The deserts of the world are full of mysteries. We may see the desert as a hot, drab, quiet place where nothing moves but wind-blown sand and the occasional lazy tarantula. But just when we think we have the desert all figured out, Death Valley surprises us with its baffling Racetrack.

153

It's the same with God. We may think we have him figured out—that we understand all about how and why he does things. But the more we study his creation, the more mysteries we find. There is a lot about God that we aren't able to understand. That's okay. That is part of who he is. Our living God is a God of action and mystery. How will he surprise us today?

Think about what God says to you

> The Lord replied, ". . . Watch and be astounded at what I will do."
>
> Habakkuk 1:5

Just when we think we have God figured out, just when we are sure we know the road that life will take, our creative God surprises us.

Let's talk to God!

MY JOURNAL (choose one)

Here are mysteries about you, God, and here's what I think they mean:

- *God is all-powerful:*

_____

_____

_____

_____

- *God is everywhere at one time:*

_____

_____

_____

_____

- *God knows everything:*

_____

_____

_____

_____

- *God is alive forever:*

_____

_____

_____

_____

MY PRAYER

Lord, sometimes I wish I could have you all figured out. But your Word tells me I never will be able to understand you fully or predict what you will do in my life. God, you are full of surprises that are good for me. Thank you for being such a great, loving, and surprising God!

Desert landscapes are some of the weirdest on Earth. Natural rock arches stretch across chasms of striped stone. Sandstone cliffs rise up out of piles of rubble. Pillars and columns of rock stand on the sands of the world's deserts like sentinels guarding treasure.

One fun desert formation is Bryce Canyon National Park in Utah. Bryce Canyon has three distinct ecosystems. The semidesert ecosystem in the lower eastern part of the park is filled with piñon trees, prairie dogs, and lizards.

Bryce Canyon cuts a dramatic gorge into a *plateau*—a high, flat stretch of land. The canyon is part of what geologists call "the Grand Staircase." Bryce Canyon is the top step. From there, a series of pink and tan cliffs slopes down to the south in giant steps until it reaches the plains where the Grand Canyon of Arizona is carved. Although much smaller than the Grand Canyon, Bryce is every bit as beautiful. It is filled with spectacular red-rock palaces, bridges, castles, and columns with descriptive names like Thor's Hammer, Wall of Windows, Fairyland Canyon, Alley Oop, Dinny the Dinosaur, Tower Bridge, and Gulliver's Castle.

How did Bryce Canyon get these amazing formations? The layers of rock

Bryce Canyonlands are some of God's finest sculptures.

156

at Bryce have different thickness and hardness. They also have vertical cracks all through them. In winter, water expands as it freezes in the cracks, breaking off pieces of rock and sculpting the elegant and graceful shapes we see today. God has sculpted the surfaces with great patience. The magnificent formations of Bryce Canyon could not have been formed overnight. It took many thousands of years of gentle erosion to wear away at the rocks in the spooky and cool way that Bryce has formed.

The process needed to happen slowly and gently, one step at a time, one winter at a time. If too much water had frozen too quickly in the cracks, Bryce Canyon would be nothing but a jumble of fallen rocks.

That's the way God operates. He uses time to change things, and sometimes he uses more time than we can imagine. We often forget that time is different to God. As the Bible says, "The Lord isn't really being slow. . . . No, he is being patient for your sake" (2 Peter 3:9).

Think about what God says to you

You must not forget, dear friends, that a day is like a thousand years to the Lord, and a thousand years is like a day.
2 Peter 3:8

Sometimes we wish God would hurry up and do what we want him to do. But we must always remember that he is using time as a tool to make things just right.

Let's talk to God!

MY JOURNAL (choose one)

Here is something that I need to be patient about, Lord:

_____

_____

_____

_____

Here is something that I know you are spending time on, God, to make it "just right" in my life:

_____

_____

_____

_____

MY PRAYER

Lord, please calm my fidgety spirit. I want to get used to your clock, not mine. I know that you sometimes take time with things, and that is hard to get used to in this hurry-up world. Thank you for using your creation to help me learn this.

Desert creatures are beautifully made for the dry life. Desert birds fly dozens of miles to oases, places where there are lakes or springs. They splash in the water, and when they fly back to the nest, their chicks drink the water in their feathers. Camels walk on the soft sand with wide hooves that keep them from sinking down, and their fatty humps help them go for a long time without liquid water. Their humps don't hold water. They hold fat, which the camel can convert into water. For a camel, carrying around a sixty-pound hump is like carrying eight gallons of fresh water! Other desert animals are furry. Their fluffy coats are like air conditioning, letting in air while keeping the hot sun out. Snakes and lizards hunt in the cool nights, and during the day they find shade in scruffy grasses. Desert plants have thick skins and small leaves to keep their water inside. Cactus plants have needles. These collect dew at night, make shade during the day, and keep hungry critters from taking a bite out of them. The needles even keep the air next to the cactus still so the cactus's skin doesn't dry out. Get the point?

God's elegant design for the desert's living things doesn't stop on the first floor. There are basement condos, too. He has given some tiny creatures the ability to live in moist soil and to hibernate when it gets dry. Single-celled protozoans feed among grains of sand during the short rainy season. When things dry up, these micro-beasties cover themselves with a coating called a cyst, under which they can remain dormant for months or even years. Tiny brine shrimp live in salty pools, laying eggs that dry out. These eggs can hatch years later,

159

as soon as they become wet again.

Let's go down even lower, into a deep crack in the dried desert mud. God made the desert snail, too. This snail hangs out during the winter months on twigs and saltbushes and lays eggs during the spring rains. But in the summer it hibernates in deep cracks of dried, baked mud. It can live several years in suspended animation. In one case, a desert snail, thought to be dead, was glued to a display in the British Museum of Natural History from March 1846 to March 1850 (that's four years for you non-math people). When somebody accidentally got it wet, it woke up and began to eat the nearby exhibit!

God has filled every crack and corner of the dry desert with life. Life thrives in the most remote, hot, cold, high, and low places of our world. God's design and care stretches to life everywhere. God is omnipresent, which is a fancy word meaning, "He's everywhere—he's everywhere!" No matter where we go, from the tops of the mountains to the bottoms of the hottest deserts, God is there.

Think about what God says to you

> "Am I not everywhere in all the heavens
> and earth?" asks the Lord.
> Jeremiah 23:24

When we look at the special ways that creatures and plants are made to live in every wacky kind of place, we see that there is no place where God is not. Life is precious to God, and he has placed it all over Earth. He has done this to bring glory to himself and to remind us that he is the God who is everywhere.

Let's talk to God!

MY JOURNAL (choose one)

This is one way that a desert animal shows how creative you are, God:

_____

_____

_____

_____

You're everywhere, God, even when I:

_____

_____

_____

_____

MY PRAYER

Dear God, Colossians 1:17 says that you existed before everything else began and that you hold all creation together. It comforts me to know that you are everywhere through time and space.

The dry valleys of Antarctica are some of the harshest places on Earth. (Photo courtesy Dale Anderson, USGS.)

It is noon in the desert. The sun has not come up for weeks, and the sky is black. Glowing curtains of green and orange light bend across the starry night; the *aurora borealis* is on display. The temperature has plummeted to ninety degrees below zero. There aren't any camels, cacti, scorpions, or tarantulas. This is not your normal desert. In fact, this is a "dry valley" in Antarctica. The largest living animal in this desert is a microscopic worm called a *nematode;* it feeds on algae in the rocks and soil. But if you're on a walk in the dry valley, you will see no signs of animal life anywhere.

There are deserts in many cold parts of our world. Like the dry valleys in Antarctica, these deserts get very little precipitation, and most of it is in the form of a few inches of snow a year. There are cold deserts in Canada, Iceland, and Russia as well. A desert doesn't have to be hot to be a desert—just dry.

From the hot Sahara in Africa to the chilled-out dry valleys of Antarctica, there are deserts all around us. It was thought for a long time that there were no living things in many of these places. There certainly were no shopping malls, so some people thought, "Why would life bother setting up camp here?" But scientists made an amazing discovery: Hiding inside rocks on the deadest looking places on Earth were whole colonies of busy bacteria. Nobody had bothered to tell them they were living in a desert, so they set up entire neighborhoods inside the rocks! These tiny creatures, called *Crytoendoliths,* live off the chemicals in the rocks. If you were buried as deep relative to your size as the Crytoendoliths are to theirs, you would be nine and a half miles beneath the surface of your rock!

The distant deserts of our world seem to be dead, at least on the surface. But there is a lot of life in those rocks! The Bible speaks of some people as having a "heart of stone," a heart so cold and hard and lifeless that they do not know God. It seems as if we can't do anything to reach these people. But God can transform the inside of a person's heart, giving it spiritual life just as he has given life to the inside of the stones in the desert. Even those of us who know God sometimes need a little more life in our hearts. In the book of Ezekiel, God promises to transform our stony hearts into tender hearts that want to obey his commands and to please him. Only God can change a human heart from the inside out!

Think about what God says to you

> I will give you a new heart with new and right desires, and I will put a new spirit in you. I will take out your stony heart of sin and give you a new, obedient heart. And I will put my Spirit in you.
> Ezekiel 36:26-27

No matter how dead and stony a heart is, God can transform it! God can give life where no life seems possible. Do you know people who, when you think about them, make you say to yourself, "They'll never become Christians—not in a million years"? Well, the more we learn about God, the more we learn to "never say never!"

Let's talk to God!

MY JOURNAL (choose one)

Lord, this is something in my life that makes me feel like I have a heart of stone:

_____

_____

_____

_____

Lord, here is someone I know who has a heart of stone when it comes to you. This is what I might do to help this person have a new heart of life:

_____

_____

_____

_____

MY PRAYER

God, you have given life to the cold, dead stones of the Antarctic desert. I know you can give life to my friends who don't know you yet. Thank you.

Camel Crossword Puzzle

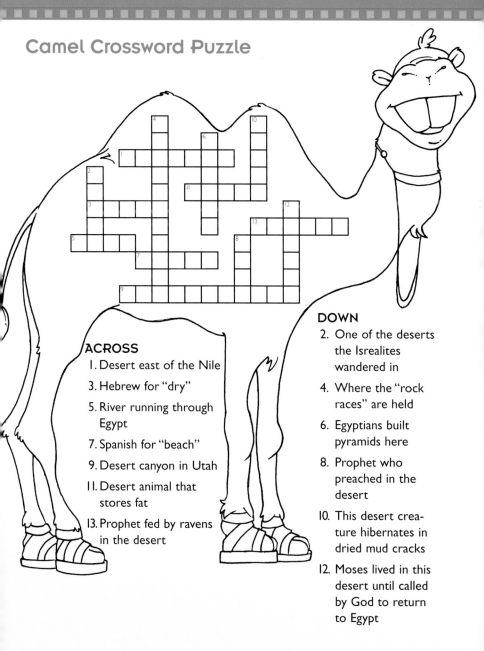

ACROSS

1. Desert east of the Nile
3. Hebrew for "dry"
5. River running through Egypt
7. Spanish for "beach"
9. Desert canyon in Utah
11. Desert animal that stores fat
13. Prophet fed by ravens in the desert

DOWN

2. One of the deserts the Isrealites wandered in
4. Where the "rock races" are held
6. Egyptians built pyramids here
8. Prophet who preached in the desert
10. This desert creature hibernates in dried mud cracks
12. Moses lived in this desert until called by God to return to Egypt

TINKERING
with God's Design

No one can discover everything
God has created in our world,
no matter how hard
they work at it.
Not even the wisest people
know everything,
even if they say they do.

Ecclesiastes 8:17

We are at the mercy of the weather. A hot, dry stretch of weather ruins crops and causes cattle to die of thirst. Then, when we least expect it, a fierce storm will sweep into a community, tearing off roofs, washing out bridges, and flooding homes and farmland. Hail falls from the sky, denting car roofs and smashing their windshields. A fork of lightning streaks out of the clouds, setting a forest ablaze. Weather causes flood, fire, and famine.

Can we do anything to control the wild roller coaster of our weather? Many scientists believe that, although we will never be able to control the weather, we can learn to modify it.

The most encouraging weather modification so far involves getting moisture out of the clouds and onto the ground. This process is called *cloud seeding*. Clouds are made up of tiny drops of water that float in the air. To seed the clouds, airplanes fly over them and drop powdered dry ice or silver iodide into the clouds. This causes the drops of water to cluster around the ice and freeze into snowflakes. The snow is too heavy to stay up, so it falls to the ground as snow or rain. This idea has also been used to "seed" hurricanes in hopes of weakening them.

One way we accidentally affect the weather is by pumping "greenhouse gases" into the air with our factories, cars, and planes. Scientists are working to reduce the production of these gases so we won't change the weather in ways that we don't want to.

Is it wise to modify the weather? Some people think we should not tinker with a powerful system that we don't really understand. They worry that we will interfere with the natural way the world is designed to work. But others believe that weather modification is a great idea and will bring rain to dry areas, stop flooding, and prevent damage and loss of life from severe storms. What do you think?

It doesn't take much to get a rainstorm going. All it takes is a little ice particle that water droplets can cluster around so they will fall onto the dry earth. Jesus came into a world that was parched and dry. He changed that world with just twelve disciples. After Jesus' death and resurrection, these twelve men scattered throughout the land. New believers clustered around them, and soon the gospel fell on the whole world like a refreshing rain!

Think about what God says to you

Jesus' death would be not for Israel only, but for the gathering together of all the children of God scattered around the world.
John 11:52

This was a new idea for the Israelites. They had always thought that the Messiah would come just to save *them*—the Jewish people. It was hard for them to believe that God cared about Gentiles, too.

Let's talk to God!

MY JOURNAL (choose one)

Lord, I'm glad for missionaries who help the gospel fall all over the world. Thank you for this missionary (these missionaries) that our church supports:

_____

_____

_____

I will encourage this missionary by:

_____

_____

_____

_____

_____

Show me, God, how to reach out to this friend who doesn't know you. I want to gather this person into my circle of Christian friends:

_____

_____

_____

_____

_____

MY PRAYER

Lord, thank you that I can make a change in the "weather" of this world when I am powered by your Spirit. Thank you for giving me a heart to change the world one person at a time. Please help me always to be kind and gentle when I tell others about my wonderful God.

Our Earth is unique. It's the only planet we know of with watery oceans sloshing around and a nice blanket of air to keep it warm at night and cool during the day. We look around at the other planets and see places that are too hot, too cold, too dry, or have air that would gag a maggot. Earth is special. It's the only place humans can live. We begin to wonder: Could we make another world more like home?

The idea of changing the environment of an entire planet is called *terraforming*. Terraforming means "to form into a likeness of Earth." Scientists believe the easiest planet to terraform would be Mars, because it is the most like Earth. Even so, Mars is cold, drier than the Sahara, and has almost no air.

It would take thousands of years and billions of dollars to change Mars into a second Earth. Though there's no liquid water on the surface, Mars may have water trapped underground. The trick is to get it out. One good way of doing this might be to put giant mirrors into orbit over Mars, which would reflect sunlight onto the polar caps of Mars to melt the ice. Icy water would melt into lakes, and frozen carbon dioxide would melt into air to thicken Mars' thin atmosphere. As the air became thicker, it would also become warmer, and more

171

ice would melt. Soon most of the water on Mars would melt. The air would be able to hold in heat like a greenhouse, and Mars would continue to warm up. This warming is called the "greenhouse effect," and it happens on Earth, too.

Then we would need factories to turn carbon dioxide into oxygen and make the atmosphere breathable. God has already invented these factories—they are live, green plants! If special plants could be grown to withstand the harsh martian environment, the entire planet could be seeded and Mars' air would become breathable. After that would come the forests, farms, and shopping malls!

Should we turn Mars into a second Earth? Those in favor of it say our population is getting too big for one planet to support, and we need to move on. Those against it say we can't treat planets as our own disposable playgrounds. When it comes to changing nature, it's good to ask: "Should we do this? Is this the right thing to do?"

Think about what God says to you

> You may say, "I am allowed to do anything."
> But I reply, "Not everything is good for you."
> 1 Corinthians 6:12

God had the apostle Paul write his friends in Corinth that just because we *can* do something doesn't mean it is a good thing to do. We must use our good sense and the leading of God's Word and Spirit to decide. There are many things that our technology makes possible. We must always ask ourselves, "Is this the *right* thing to do?" The Bible doesn't talk about terraforming, so we need to figure it out responsibly, asking God for his wisdom.

Let's talk to God!

MY JOURNAL (choose one)

This is something that I am allowed to do, but because I love you, Lord, I choose not to:

_____

_____

_____

_____

This is why I think terraforming Mars is the right thing to do, God:

_____

_____

_____

_____

This is why I think terraforming Mars is the wrong thing to do, God:

_____

_____

_____

_____

MY PRAYER

Lord, help me always to make wise decisions. Many things in life are allowed, but not everything is good for me. Help me decide to do the things that will show people your love and goodness, and help me respect and care for the creation that you have put around me.

You are not a clone. Even if you are an identical twin, you have a mix of genes from both your parents. A clone has only one parent. It is identical to that parent in every way because it has exactly the same set of genes. Did you know that cloning happens in nature? The sea anemone can reproduce by splitting in two. Farmers cut shoots off banana trees to start new trees. The new little tree is a clone: it has exactly the same genes as its parent tree.

Laboratory cloning is the science of trying to change and control the design of living things. For example, scientists can take a section of the genes from one plant that resists a certain disease and put it into another plant to make it resist the disease too. Or genes from a very healthy animal can be added to the genes of an animal that tends to get sick to make it more healthy. Scientists are able to clone bacteria, plants, mice, sheep, and pigs.

This is how scientists cloned the famous sheep Dolly: They took all the genetic information out of an unfertilized egg cell from a sheep. Then they joined this "empty" cell with another cell from a second female sheep and put it into the womb of a third female sheep. Soon, a little lamb named Dolly was born, a clone of the second sheep. There were 276 failures before the success of Dolly. Dolly herself died at a young age. Scientists are not sure why.

One goal of cloning animals is to raise healthier and larger animals that we can use for food. Another goal is to clone animals for medical use. Research to cure disease could possibly go much faster using cloned animals. Animals could also be used in human medical transplants. Human genes would be added to the animal's genes to make the transplant organs more easily accepted by the human body. The sick person would not have to wait years for a human liver, heart, or kidney, which would save many human lives.

Some people think that this kind of cloning is a good idea because it will help sick people. Others feel that it is not a good plan and that using animals in this way is not a responsible way to treat God's creatures. Whatever decision is made, we must be careful of how and why we use animals for people's health. What do you think?

Think about what God says to you

> Not even a sparrow, worth only half a penny,
> can fall to the ground without your Father knowing it.
> And the very hairs on your head are all numbered.
> So don't be afraid; you are more valuable
> to him than a whole flock of sparrows.
> Matthew 10:29-31

The Bible makes it clear that God places a high value on human life. Think about someone you love very much. Now imagine that somehow you could love that person a hundred times as much as you do right now. Guess what? God loves you even more than that!

Let's talk to God!

MY JOURNAL

In the verses about the sparrows, this is what I hear you saying to me, God:

_____

_____

_____

_____

_____

MY PRAYER

Dear God, it comforts me to know how much you value my life. You even numbered each and every hair on my head!

DAY 4: EMBRYOS ARE PEOPLE TOO

Scientists are learning how to change the gene structure in people. In your lifetime you will be able to make decisions that your grandparents never dreamed of and your parents only imagined. Because of new genetic engineering technology, by the time you and your husband or wife are ready to have a baby, you may be able to have it custom-made. Perhaps you will order a boy or a girl, choose the hair and eye color, and take away any flawed genetic characteristics.

Scientists are working to duplicate—or clone—human embryos, which would provide some of the same benefits as cloned animals. Cloned embryos would make genetic research easier and cheaper. These embryos could provide healthy organs for people who need transplants. Cloning could also give children to infertile or homosexual couples and could provide an identical replacement for a lost loved one. But President Clinton placed a temporary ban on using federal money for human cloning research. He said, "Any discovery that touches upon human creation is not simply a matter of scientific inquiry; it is a matter of morality and spirituality as well." Private companies in America, however, are allowed to do human cloning research.

Many Christians think human cloning is not pleasing to God. Human beings are not laboratory mice—they are God's creation. God created each of us to be unique—one of a kind. God created

177

each of us to be priceless, not a product to be ordered, manufactured, and modified like a piece of furniture. God also designed marriage so that children could be born into a loving home with a mom and a dad, not grown in a laboratory. Cloning is also dangerous—it took 276 failures before the successful cloning of the sheep Dolly. Each human embryo and fetus is precious to God. How many hundreds would have to die to achieve one successful clone?

When do we cross over the line of being good stewards of God's creation and start trying to be God? That happens when we decide to create human life in laboratories. God is the Creator; scientists can only copy. The Bible doesn't teach us that science is bad. Science has a lot to offer us, and it helps us as Christians learn more about God and how his creation works. When we are faced with new questions about right and wrong in the world of science, there are things we can do to help us decide what stand to take. We can see what the Bible says about God and his relationship to us and to the world around us. We can ask him to give us his wisdom. We can talk to other believers about what their stand is and why they believe what they believe. Then we can act in a way that will bring the world to God and his message of salvation.

Think about what God says to you

> *We are God's masterpiece. He has created us anew in Christ Jesus, so that we can do the good things he planned for us long ago.*
> *Ephesians 2:10*

A masterpiece is an outstanding craft or work of art. Did you know that you are a beautiful work of art created by God? God does not turn out junk, and he doesn't have to practice to get things right. As a child of God, you have his divine stamp on you that says, "Original, one-of-a-kind work of art. Signed, God."

Let's talk to God!

MY JOURNAL (choose one)

Lord, there are times when I don't feel like a masterpiece. Help me to remember I'm your one-of-a-kind creation when:

_____

_____

_____

_____

This is someone I trust, Lord, to help me figure out what stand to take on human cloning:

_____

_____

_____

_____

This is how I think you must feel about genetic engineering, God:

_____

_____

_____

_____

MY PRAYER

Dear Lord, please help me to be wise as I try to figure out what to believe about all the new advances in science. Please give your wisdom to scientists in the field of genetics and cloning. Help them not to try to take your place as the Creator.

The most powerful force ever discovered is contained within the tiniest thing imaginable—the nucleus of an atom! In the 1940s scientists learned how to split the atom, a division which causes a chain reaction of released energy. When this chain reaction is uncontrolled, the result is a huge explosion. This energy was first used as a weapon in the atom bomb, dropped on Japan at the end of World War II. When the chain reaction of released nuclear energy is controlled, its power can be used for more peaceful purposes. Nuclear-powered ships, nuclear submarines, and nuclear power plants are examples of this.

Until the 1970s most of the industrial countries of the world used coal to run their power plants. But coal-burning electric plants were polluting the air. Also, the coal mines began to run out of coal. The world's population was growing so fast that the power companies couldn't provide enough electricity. There was a need to find a new way to generate electricity. So scientists and engineers invented nuclear power plants. Today there are 110 nuclear power plants in the United States alone, providing 20 percent of our electricity.

Nuclear power plants make electricity by boiling water. The energy to boil the water is created by splitting uranium atoms deep in the nuclear reactor's core. This causes tremendous heat, which boils the water, causing steam. The steam powers the turbine, which makes electricity. Sounds perfect, doesn't it?

But if the reactor isn't kept cool enough, there can be an explosion and a meltdown, with radiation released into the air. Radiation can make people very sick and can even kill them. In 1979 a nuclear reactor meltdown occurred at Three Mile Island, Pennsylvania. A much worse explosion and meltdown occurred in 1986 in Chernobyl, Ukraine. Five thousand people died, and many others are still sick from the radiation.

Many people think that nuclear energy is not safe and that we need to look for other ways to make energy. Others say that we know enough now to design and run much safer nuclear reactors. What do you think we should do?

Power needs to be used wisely. As human beings learn how to make power in new ways, they will make mistakes. But God never makes mistakes. He is so powerful that even if you split every atom on this earth, it would not equal his power. How thankful we can be that God is always wise in using his unlimited power!

Think about what God says to you

You are the God of miracles and wonders! You demonstrate your awesome power among the nations.
Psalm 77:14

God designed the universe, and he designed the atom. His power lives in even the tiniest pieces of his creation.

Let's talk to God!

MY JOURNAL (choose one)

Lord, I think that this is a wise use of the nuclear power that you have made available to us:

_____

_____

_____

_____

Lord, I think that you never planned for people to use nuclear power in this way:

_____

_____

_____

_____

MY PRAYER

Dear God, thank you for reminding me that you are infinite in your power.

WORD SEARCH

```
Y  C  O  L  P  O  Q  N  G  E  N  E  T  I  C
T  S  W  T  X  C  L  O  N  I  N  G  W  S  E
I  O  Y  R  B  M  E  J  P  U  K  O  I  F  N
C  A  B  D  E  F  A  G  H  W  I  N  H  U  G
I  C  R  E  A  T  O  R  O  I  L  U  T  R  I
R  S  N  T  O  U  S  Y  S  S  E  C  B  E  N
T  O  H  M  T  W  E  W  I  D  L  L  L  H  E
C  R  G  E  T  H  E  R  S  O  P  E  N  T  E
E  G  A  D  E  N  A  T  H  M  O  A  S  A  R
L  A  O  U  N  P  A  D  T  H  W  R  F  E  I
E  N  I  R  A  M  B  U  S  U  E  Y  I  W  N
A  S  T  T  E  R  R  A  F  O  R  M  I  N  G
```

FIND THESE HIDDEN WORDS:

ATOM	ENGINEERING	SHEEP
CLONING	GENETIC	SUBMARINE
CREATOR	MARS	TERRAFORMING
ELECTRICITY	NUCLEAR	WEATHER
EMBRYO	ORGAN	WISDOM
	POWER	

Net Search

Use the Internet to find out more about the topics we've looked at this week. Here are some key words to help you get started: weather modification, Mars terraforming, nuclear power plants, cloning.

For the
BIRDS

God said, . . . "Let the sky
be filled with birds
of every kind."

Genesis 1:20

Doves and pigeons are closely related members of the same bird family—*Columbidae,* if you must know! In science books, doves are described as "gentle, amorous, and monogamous." That means that they are affectionate to their mates and faithful to one mate their whole lives. They have a soft, pleasant, cooing call.

Doves and pigeons are mentioned in the Bible more than any other birds. They were used by the Israelites for food and for religious sacrifices because they were ritually clean animals. The dove was the most common sacrifice offered by the poor, since it cost less to buy than a goat or a lamb.

Doves were domesticated in the Near East long before most other birds. In fact, pictures of domesticated rock doves show up in Egyptian art from as long ago as 3100 B.C. Doves were used as carriers to send messages from one place to another. That gives new meaning to the words "air mail"!

Now that we understand more about the role of the dove in the ancient Near East, it makes a lot of sense that Noah would send a dove as a messenger to the outside world. "Is it safe to come out of the ark yet?" was the question Noah asked. What good news it was when that little dove came back clutching a fresh olive leaf in its beak!

Think about what God says to you

Then he sent out a dove to see if it could find dry ground. But the dove found no place to land because the water was still too high. So it returned to the boat, and Noah held out his hand and drew the dove back inside. Seven days later, Noah released the dove again. This time, toward evening, the bird returned to him with a fresh olive leaf in its beak. Noah now knew that the water was almost gone. A week later, he released the dove again, and this time it did not come back.

Genesis 8:8-12

Like the dove in the story of Noah, we can be God's messengers to the outside world.

Let's talk to God!

MY JOURNAL

This is a quality that the dove has that I would like to have too, God:

_____

_____

_____

_____

MY PRAYER

Dear Lord, thank you for the stories of the dove in your Word. I want to be your messenger and carry the good news of the gospel to others. I may fly over the ocean, travel across distant deserts, or stay close to home. But wherever you send me, I want to keep the symbol of the dove in mind as I do your work.

Fill me with the Holy Spirit, which you sent down in the form of a dove to Jesus when he was baptized.

Help me to stay faithful to you, as the dove is faithful to its mate.

Teach me to be gentle as a dove with others.

Like Noah's dove, let me share the gospel of peace, symbolized by the olive leaf. Please let the words that come out of my mouth be peaceful.

DAY 2: THE RAVEN

The glossy black raven, which is the largest member of the crow family, can be two feet long from beak to tail. It is a scavenger that lives just about everywhere north of the equator. It can be tamed and can learn to copy human speech. Many ornithologists (scientists who study birds) think that the raven is the most intelligent of all the birds. However, it has an unpleasant caw that sounds like a rusty hinge.

In the story of Noah's ark, at first it seems like the dove has the glamorous role. By not returning to the ark, she gave the sign that it was time to disembark. But if you think about it, God gave the raven a part to play that was every bit as important as the dove's. The message of the raven was, "Don't get out of the boat yet. Not yet. Think about it. Wait on God's perfect timing." Although the water was receding, there was still no vegetation; there were no plants growing for the animals to eat and no trees for the birds to nest in. Poor Noah and his family spent an entire year cooped up in that ark full of noisy, smelly animals, waiting for God's sign that it was time to leave the ark.

The raven is featured in another Bible story, too. Israel's godless King Ahab and his evil wife, Queen Jezebel, worshiped idols. The prophet Elijah told them that because of this, God would not send any rain for three years. That really made them mad, so God told

Elijah to go and hide in the east. While Elijah was hiding and waiting, God sent ravens to bring him food twice a day. The message the ravens brought Elijah, along with the bread and meat, was, "God won't abandon you during this time."

Isn't waiting the hardest thing to do? But the waiting is easier when we know, like Noah and Elijah did, that God is wise. He will give us what we need when we need it. It's tough learning to wait—to do things in God's time and not our own. Yet we learn a lot about ourselves—and about God—as we learn to wait and listen to him in those quiet times.

Think about what God says to you

After another forty days, Noah opened the window he had made in the boat and released a raven that flew back and forth until the earth was dry.
Genesis 8:6-7

Maybe you can be a "raven" in someone's life. Maybe you can encourage a friend not to be in a hurry to grow up, not to start dating too early, not to try everything new. "Wait," says the raven. And in this fast-food, instant-gratification world, that's an important word.

Let's talk to God!

MY JOURNAL (choose one)

God, this is an area in my life where I have to wait, and I don't under-
stand why:

_____

_____

_____

_____

God, this is a time when I decided to wait for something, and I'm glad I
did because:

_____

_____

_____

_____

MY PRAYER

Dear God, I sometimes feel like I'm being pulled two ways. The world says
GO, but I know I hear your voice saying STOP. I want to learn how to live
my life in your timing. I want to live a life that isn't hurried, pressured,
stressed, or out of control. Teach me through your Word and through the
advice of wise family and friends how to follow your timing and walk in
step with you. As I learn to accept your timing, give me a chance to
encourage my friends to stop, think, and wait on you also. Help me
explain that you want to show them not just what to do, but when to
do it.

DAY 3: THE TRIUMPHANT TRUMPETER SWAN

One hundred and fifty years ago, beautiful white trumpeter swans were a common sight from South Carolina all the way up to Alaska, migrating in huge flocks each fall and spring. Their clear, trumpetlike calls carried across the air for more than a mile.

Hunted by eagles and coyotes, the trumpeter swans still thrived in numbers too big to count until the American population grew and pioneers moved west. Tired of eating buffalo meat, the settlers hunted swans. They found that, besides tasting delicious, the swans had soft down that was ideal for stuffing quilts and feather beds. Their strong quills were perfect for making pens, and their skins brought a good price. Wealthy people paid fifty dollars for a pair of trumpeter swans to swim in their ornamental ponds. Soon, the swans were almost gone.

In 1918 a Bird Treaty ended all hunting of the swans, but it was nearly too late. In 1935 there were only seventy-three trumpeter swans left in the United States. The National Wildlife Federation took action, raising money to develop a trumpeter swan refuge at Red Rock, Montana.

Now the swans can breed in safety. They build huge nests, six feet across, out of marsh plants. One of their favorite building sites is on top of a muskrat house! The female swan lays from two to ten eggs, which she and her mate guard carefully until the cygnets (baby swans) hatch in June. The cygnets head straight for the water to spend the warm summer splashing and growing. In October they are ready to learn to fly.

Something interesting has happened to the swans over the last hundred years. They no longer migrate, and no one is sure why. As in the movie *Fly Away Home*, scientists and conservationists are working with some of the cygnets, getting them used to the sound of an airplane before they even hatch, and teaching them to migrate by following the plane. Scientists hope they can reintroduce the swans into territory they inhabited long ago.

Today there are twenty thousand trumpeter swans in refuges in Alaska and the western United States. Do you ever feel like you need a refuge?

Think about what God says to you

> The Lord is a shelter for the oppressed,
> a refuge in times of trouble.
> Psalm 9:9

Kind of feel like life is too much for you? Try this: Go to a quiet spot where you can be alone with God. Talk to him there about how you feel. Ask him to be your refuge. He will do it. Always remember, you serve a mighty God who loves you and is there for you.

Let's talk to God!

MY JOURNAL

God, I will ask you to be my refuge when:

_____

_____

_____

_____

MY PRAYER

Dear God, thank you for loving me and always being there for me when I need a refuge from life's troubles. I'm glad to know that you will be my refuge forever.

Ridiculous Bird Riddles!

Q. Which side of a swan has the most feathers?
A. The outside.

Q. Why did the eagle put a desk in the tree?
A. He wanted to open a branch office.

Q. What do you get when a canary flies into a blender?
A. Shredded tweet.

Q. What do you get when you cross a chicken with a cement mixer?
A. A brick layer.

Q. What do you get when you cross a parakeet with a cat?
A. A peeping tom.

Q. What do you get when you cross a parrot with an alligator?
A. A pet that bites your hand off and says, "Who's a pretty boy now?"

Q. What do you get when you cross a raven with a hippopotamus?
A. A lot of broken telephone wires.

Bonus Riddle

Q. Why can't a polar bear ever catch a penguin?
A. Polar bears live at the North Pole, and penguins live at the South Pole.

DAY 4: THE AMERICAN BALD EAGLE

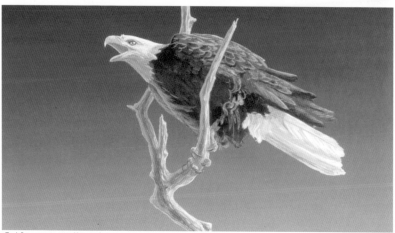

God frees us to soar like eagles.

Bald eagles are found in North America and nowhere else. They're the national bird of the United States. They mate for life and may live up to thirty years in the wild. They almost became extinct because of hunting, loss of habitat, and their biggest enemy, the pesticide DDT. DDT worked its way up the food chain until it reached the eagles, which began laying eggs that were so thin they broke before the chicks could hatch. Fortunately DDT was banned in 1972. With careful conservation, the birds began to multiply, and in July 2000 they were taken off the endangered species list! Today there are fifty thousand bald eagles. Although they are found as far south as northern Mexico, 80 percent of them live in Alaska. Bald eagles have seven thousand feathers arranged in outer and inner layers that insulate and waterproof them. This allows them to live comfortably in Alaska's cold climate.

The bald eagle is a hunter like no other. Think you've got good eyesight? The bald eagle can spot a fish in the water from several hundred feet in the air. It can see a mouse moving on the ground from two thousand feet up in the air and a rabbit from almost a mile away. Its eyesight is four times stronger than any human's. To see as well as a bald eagle does, you'd have to use a strong pair of binoculars!

Even more amazing than its eyesight is the bald eagle's flying ability. God gave the eagle wide, long wings to soar with. A full-grown bald eagle has a six-foot wingspan. Its wing feathers are hollow and lightweight but very strong and flexible. The bald eagle rides the waves of thermals (warm updrafts of air) like the finest surfer alive. When it spots a fish or a rabbit, the bald eagle goes into a power dive, using its strong tail as a rudder and a brake. If you get the chance to see a bald eagle sailing through the air high above you, you'll find that it's a glorious sight you'll never forget.

God has given the eagle the power to soar to great heights, along with the strength and eyesight to be a magnificent hunter. In the same way, God has given us the strength to rise above life's difficulties.

Think about what God says to you

> *Those who wait on the Lord will find new strength.*
> *They will fly high on wings like eagles. They will run*
> *and not grow weary. They will walk and not faint.*
>
> Isaiah 40:31

This verse is a promise to you from God. He means every word of it. It doesn't matter how tired or worn down or discouraged you are. If you patiently trust him to keep his promise, he will fill you with strength. He will lift you up above your despair. You will soar!

Let's talk to God!

MY JOURNAL (choose one)

God, this is one difficulty that I'd like to ask you to lift me above:

_____

_____

_____

_____

This is how I felt one time when you lifted me, Lord:

_____

_____

_____

_____

MY PRAYER

Dear God, I do get tired and sad sometimes. But I trust your Word when it tells me you are even stronger than my discouragement. You will give me the strength I need from your own storehouse of strength.

DAY 5: THE EMPEROR PENGUIN—DEVOTED DAD

Antarctica—it's a rough place to be a bird! The coldest temperature ever recorded on Earth was -126.9 degrees Fahrenheit during an Antarctic winter. The average temperature at the South Pole is -56.7 degrees Fahrenheit. But it's home to the seventeen species of penguins that live there, one of which is shown above.

God designed penguins to be world-class swimmers and divers, but they can't fly. Their wings are like flippers, and they use their webbed feet as rudders. They zip through the icy water at twenty miles per hour as they hunt fish, squid, and shrimp. This speed also comes in handy when they themselves are being hunted by killer whales and leopard seals! On land, penguins are slow and have to waddle or hop. Their favorite method of land travel is tobogganing. They slide along on their bellies, pushing with their flippers and reaching top speeds of half a mile per hour. No wonder they love the water!

Of the seventeen types of penguins, the emperor penguin is the most unusual. The emperor penguin is the biggest kind of penguin, growing up to four feet tall. It is also the least affected by the cold and does not migrate to warmer areas during the winter as the other Antarctic animals do. It is the only penguin that breeds and hatches eggs in the winter.

The female emperor penguin lays one egg in June, which is the middle of the winter in Antarctica. Then she takes off for nine weeks to fatten up on fish and shrimp, leaving the male to incubate the egg. All the males in the rookery huddle together for warmth, each one carefully cradling the precious egg on top of his webbed feet to keep it off the cold ice. A special flap below his stomach keeps the egg warm. If the egg hatches before the female returns, the male regurgitates a curdlike substance to feed the chick, still cuddling on top of his feet. When Mom does come back and regurgitates fish for the little tike, the male penguin takes a few weeks off to go fatten up in the water. Then together they care for the chick until it is ready to hunt for its own food.

Like the male emperor penguin, your father, grandfather, uncle, or big brother works very hard to teach you, protect you, take care of you, and provide for you. You don't have to stand on his feet like the baby penguins do, but you can sit at his feet and really listen to him when he is telling a story or teaching you something new.

Think about what God says to you

Listen to your father, who gave you life.... O my son, give me your heart. May your eyes delight in my ways of wisdom.
Proverbs 23:22, 26

Your father wants to teach you. He knows things that will help you later in life, like how to take care of the car, how to play chess, how to work hard, and how to know the Lord better. Even if it's something that doesn't seem very interesting or important to you right now, it pleases God when you listen to your dad and learn what he is trying to teach you.

Let's talk to God!

MY JOURNAL (choose one)

My dad (grandpa, uncle, big brother) taught me this, and it really meant a lot, God:

_____

_____

_____

_____

This is one thing I will do, Lord, to let my dad know I appreciate him:

_____

_____

_____

_____

MY PRAYER

Dear God, thank you for giving me my dad (or someone to take his place if he can't always be around). I still have many things to learn!

Cook Up Some Winter Bird Pudding

Birds really appreciate a little extra food during the winter!

TO MAKE THE PUDDING YOU WILL NEED:

- an empty margarine tub or yogurt container
- a hole punch
- a piece of string
- a Popsicle stick
- glue
- fat scraps from the grocery meat department (They're free, but it's a good idea to call ahead and have the butcher save some for you.)
- kitchen scraps
- a saucepan of hot water
- a smaller pan or bowl to set in the hot water

WHAT TO DO:

Punch a hole in the rim of the container and tie one end of the string to it so you can hang the pudding from a tree branch. Now glue the Popsicle stick to the other side of the rim from the string so half of it is sticking out of the container. This will give the birds a place to perch while they eat. Let the glue dry.

Have your mom or dad heat some water just to boiling in a saucepan on the stove, then turn off the heat. Now put the fat scraps in a small heatproof bowl and set that in the saucepan of hot water. Stir the fat around as it melts. When it is melted, mix in any kitchen scraps you have: pieces of apple, a handful of oats, stale bread, or crackers. Then pour the "bird pudding" into the tub, leaving an inch of room at the top. When the pudding hardens, you can hang your feeder in a tree. The birds will thank you!

CREEPY
Crawlies

**Your crops will be abundant,
for I will guard them
from insects and disease.**

Malachi 3:11

When was the last time you were bitten by a mosquito or stung by a bee? Do you remember swatting at an annoying fly, battling a battalion of ants marching across the kitchen floor, or wrestling a flea collar onto your unhappy cat? What were you muttering at the time? Probably something like this: "These nasty bugs. I just hate 'em!" Bugs have a reputation for being nothing but swarming, stinging, creepy disease-carriers. But the next time you start to pick up a spray can of Raid® to continue the battle, consider this: God made bugs.

Okay. The question would be *why?* Why would God create fleas that spread the dreaded Black Plague in the Middle Ages? Why would he create mosquitoes that carry malaria and yellow fever, and tsetse flies that give people sleeping sickness? What about ticks that give us Lyme disease? And cockroaches? Don't even get me started on them!

Just for a minute, let's imagine a world without bugs. Here you are in our bugless world. What's the first thing you notice? You realize how quiet it is. No crickets chirping, no flies buzzing, and no birds singing. What, no birds? That's right. There are no birds because there are no insects for them to eat. You wander over to a nearby pond. No fish. That's right. No fish to eat, because there are no insects to feed the fish. In fact, bugs are on the very important bottom rung of the food chain. In our imaginary bug-free world there are no snakes or lizards or bears or . . . hey! Where did all the flowers go? There aren't any fruit trees in this world either. In fact, there is not very much to eat at all.

Bugs can be a trial, no doubt about it. But they are part of God's intelligent design for our world. The good news is there won't be any bugs in heaven. Come to think of it, there won't be any troubles or irritations of any kind. Yay! But while you are here on earth you can expect all kinds of aggravation, from things like running out of lead for your mechanical pencil during a big test to running out of ideas on how to get along with your sister. Why not take a few minutes and ask God what he wants you to learn in the midst of this. Can what's bugging you bear fruit and help you grow?

Think about what God says to you

[Jesus said,] "Here on earth you will have many trials and sorrows. But take heart, because I have overcome the world."

John 16:33

205

Way back when Jesus was living here on earth, he knew about the things that would be bugging you today. But Jesus also knew that he was going to die and live again, overcoming Satan's ability to be the final victor. Because of Jesus, the trials and sorrows you may be facing right now are only temporary. Jesus is your "overcomer."

Let's talk to God!

MY JOURNAL

This is what's bugging me most right now, God:

_____

_____

_____

_____

This is what I think you might want me to learn from it:

_____

_____

_____

_____

MY PRAYER

Dear God, help me to look to you for wisdom not just in the big, dramatic troubles in my life, but also in the little things that bug me. You can use anything to teach me!

Tongue Twister

Bet you can't say this three times in a row:
Blue bugs bleed black blood, but black bugs bleed blue blood.

Today's story sounds like a science fiction movie, but it's really true. In 1956 a researcher brought African killer bees to Brazil to study. The next year twenty-six colonies of the bees escaped from the research facility and bred with local European honeybees. The resulting bees were called Africanized honeybees. They slowly spread through South America, up through Central America, and in 1990 they reached Texas. In 1994 they arrived in California, and someday they are expected to spread through most of the southern United States. They don't do well in cold weather, so the hope is that they won't invade the northern states. Scientists, farmers, and beekeepers are monitoring their progress, destroying hives when they can.

Everyone wants to prevent these bees from breeding with honeybees in the United States, and here's why: Honeybees are very helpful to humans. They have been domesticated for honey production, and they are also used to pollinate crops, boosting the agricultural production in the U.S. by $10 billion per year. When honeybees breed with Africanized honeybees, the resulting bees are not good crop pollinators, and they produce less honey than regular honeybees.

Although Africanized honeybees look like regular bees and their sting is no more dangerous, they are very unpredictable. They are ten times more likely to sting when they feel threatened. They tend to swarm on animals or people who get near their hives. They will chase the "threat" for a quarter of a mile or more to sting it. Because of their fierceness and unpredictability, they are almost impossible for beekeepers to manage.

When we team up with unbelievers, just as with honeybees and "killer bees," the result is unpredictable. That is why God tells us in his Word not to partner with unbelievers. This doesn't mean we should choose only Christian friends or that we should avoid non-Christians. Not at all. We can show non-Christians God's love in many ways. But the Bible is clear that we should not go into partnerships with unbelievers, whether in business or in marriage (2 Corinthians 6:14-15). When we marry, we please God when we choose to marry a fellow Christian. Otherwise, as we learned above, the results will be unpredictable. Our husband or wife might someday become a believer, but then again, he or she might not. We might find ourselves moving away from our close relationship with God. There might be confusion and arguments about what to teach our children about God.

Think about what God says to you

> Don't team up with those who are unbelievers.
> How can goodness be a partner with wickedness?
> How can light live with darkness? What harmony can there be between Christ and the Devil? How can a believer be a partner with an unbeliever? And what union can there be between God's temple and idols?
>
> 2 Corinthians 6:14-16

We live in the world right next to a lot of unbelievers. We love them and care about them, and we share the Good News about Jesus with them. But this verse warns us not to get so involved with them that it hurts our relationship with God.

Let's talk to God!

MY JOURNAL (choose one)

God, this is why I think you wouldn't want me to go into partnership with an unbeliever:

_____

_____

_____

_____

This is why I think you wouldn't want me to marry an unbeliever:

_____

_____

_____

_____

This is one way I can show your love to an unbeliever:

_____

_____

_____

_____

MY PRAYER

Dear God, you tell me not to team up with unbelievers. I know you say this to guide me so that I can keep my freedom in you, so that I don't get pulled in two different directions, and so that my life can be spent loving you and enjoying you. If you want me to get married someday, I know you will help me find a wonderful Christian to marry. I'll wait for your best and not be tempted to marry the first person who comes along.

The long-legged, black desert ant lives in a sea of sameness—sand as far as her little eyes can see. Only half an inch long, the desert ant of Tunisia is known for her speed and hardiness. Summer temperatures on the sand can get up to 160 degrees Fahrenheit. Heat is no problem for this little gal. The hot sun is her friend; it kills less rugged insects. As the sun bakes down on the sand, the ant scurries out of her burrow to find the tasty fried morsels of other insects and drag them back home to share with her colony.*

The hunting ant runs at top speed, often traveling two hundred yards from her burrow looking for food. That's like thirteen miles to us. There aren't very many landmarks in the sand, and sandstorms frequently change the shape of the landscape. So what gives? How does she find her way home? Scientists have studied this ant for several years, and now they have the answer.

God designed this ant with a thousand lenses in each eye. Humans have only one. Eighty of the lenses in each of the ant's eyes are specially designed to note the polarization of the sun's ultraviolet rays in different parts of the sky. The most intense polarization is always ninety degrees away from the sun. That's why rainbows are always on

*DID YOU KNOW THAT 99.9% OF ALL ANTS ARE FEMALE?

the opposite side of the sky from the sun. The little ant uses this "sun map" to navigate back to her home.

The desert ant navigates by the sun. We navigate by God the Son, Jesus. Following him keeps us on track, however far we may get from home.

Think about what God says to you

[Zechariah said,] "Because of God's tender mercy,
the light from heaven is about to break upon us,
to give light to those who sit in darkness and in the shadow of
death, and to guide us to the path of peace."

Luke 1:78-79

When John the Baptist was born, his father, Zechariah, praised God and prophesied about Jesus' coming with these words. That light he talked about—the Light of the World—is here, and he is the perfect guidance system. Keep your eyes on him and you can't go wrong!

Let's talk to God!

MY JOURNAL (choose one)

Lord, there was a time when I didn't keep my eyes on you. I felt like I was sitting "in darkness" and didn't know which way to go when:

_____

_____

_____

_____

I'm glad, Lord, that you lead me on "the path of peace" when:

_____

_____

_____

_____

Jesus, I know you are "the light from heaven" because:

_____

_____

_____

_____

MY PRAYER

Dear God, thank you so much for sending Jesus to be my light. I will keep my eyes on him and follow where he leads me.

Bug Joke

Biologist: What's six inches long, is yellow with black spots, and crawls?
Lab Assistant: What?
Biologist: I don't know, but it's crawling up your pant leg.

DAY 4: THE SCORPION

This guy is one tough arachnid! The scorpion survived and thrived during the age of dinosaurs, their extinction, and on through the Ice Ages. It is part of the arachnid family because it has eight legs like a spider does. It has two sets of pincers and a poisonous tail with a stinger, and it carries this tail like a curved spear arched up over its back.

The scorpion likes it hot! Most of the world's thirteen hundred species of scorpions live in hot, dry parts of the world. Ninety species live in the deserts of Arizona in the United States. Scorpions are also found in the Sahara Desert and in the deserts of Australia, while some live in Central and South America in hot, wet places.

Most scorpions hunt at night, eating insects, other scorpions, lizards, snakes, and mice. Their natural enemies are bats, tarantulas, and owls. The elf owl of the Arizona desert is probably the best scorpion hunter of all. It swoops down and nips off the scorpion's stinger, then has a nice dinner!

It is easy to find a scorpion in the dark if you happen to have an ultraviolet lamp—it has a substance in its body that is fluorescent. But unless you are a scientist and really know what you're doing, it's best not to go scorpion hunting.

The scorpion's poison is made up of neurotoxins, which affect the victim's nervous system. In the rare case when a very poisonous species of scorpion stings a person, the severe pain and swelling from the sting are followed by numbness, frothing at the mouth, difficulty breathing, and convulsions. These days people rarely die from scorpion stings because scientists have developed an antivenin that stops the paralyzing effect of the neurotoxins.

The world's most dangerous scorpions live in Africa's Sahara Desert and in the Middle East. In fact, Moses talks about them in Deuteronomy 8:15: "Do not forget that [the Lord] led you through the great and terrifying wilderness with poisonous snakes and scorpions, where it was so hot and dry." Moses used scorpions as a symbol of something harmful to show that God will lovingly protect us from many dangers.

Think about what God says to you

You fathers—if your children ask for a fish, do you give them a snake instead? Or if they ask for an egg, do you give them a scorpion? Of course not! If you sinful people know how to give good gifts to your children, how much more will your heavenly Father give the Holy Spirit to those who ask him.
Luke 11:11-13

God is your perfect parent. He would never give you anything that would be bad for you. He loves to answer your prayers, to bless you, and to fill you with the gift of the Holy Spirit.

Let's talk to God!

MY JOURNAL (choose one)
This is a danger that worries me a lot, God, so I need you to protect me from it:

_____

_____

_____

_____

This is a gift that I'm very glad you give to me, heavenly Father:

_____

_____

_____

_____

MY PRAYER

Dear God, thank you for giving me my parents, who love and protect me. It's good to be reminded that you love me even more than they do and can protect me from things that scare me.

Scorpion News Flash

The lethal toxin scorpions use to paralyze and kill their prey is helping to treat a deadly type of brain cancer. This cancer is called glioblastoma, *and up until now it has been impossible to treat. Even if the original tumor is removed by surgery, the cancer spreads to other parts of the brain. If doctors use radiation, it does too much damage to the healthy parts of the brain. And chemotherapy drugs can't be used because the molecules in the drugs are too big to cross the blood-brain barrier.*

The cells in this cancer put out chloride and water so they can shrink and move into new areas of the brain. But here's the good news. Scientists have been able to copy scorpion toxin. When it is injected, this chlorotoxin goes straight to the cancer cells and blocks the channels in the cells that put out the chloride and water, so the cancer cells can't shrink and travel through the brain. Hooray for scorpion toxin!

The spider has been around since dinosaur times, and maybe even before that. The spider and the scorpion are members of the arachnid family. Spider blood is green or pale blue, not red like ours. The spider can walk on the ceiling because it has special tufts of hair at the end of each of its eight legs. Its body is divided into two parts. The front part is the *cephalothorax* and the back part is the *abdomen*.

Most of the forty thousand species of spiders are harmless and even helpful. Lots of them eat pests like flies and mosquitoes. But two spider species in the United States give spiders a bad reputation: the brown recluse and the black widow. Drop for drop, their venom is more concentrated than a rattlesnake's!

The brown recluse is golden brown and sometimes has a darker brown abdomen. Its venom is a cell-eating chemical, not a neurotoxin like the black widow's and most other spiders' venom. The black widow is a big, fat, shiny black spider with a red hourglass on the underside of her abdomen. She gets her name from her lovely habit of sometimes gobbling up her mate. Only the female black widow is poisonous. She usually spins her webs in garages, window wells, and bushes. If you think you see a brown recluse or black widow, go get your mom or dad right away. Don't try to kill the spider yourself.

The spider is famous for its ability to spin webs to catch its prey. At the bottom of the spider's abdomen are three spinnerets, which put out the fine silk the spider uses. Spider silk is so thin that it has been used for the cross-hairs on some optical instruments. The most familiar spiderwebs are the circular orb webs we see. The orb-weaving spider can spin a web in about an hour, using one hundred yards of silk. The spider starts out with a single silk thread, dropping down from what will be the top of the web. It waits until a breeze gives it a ride over to the next anchor point. After it has the basic frame, or outline for the web, it spins spokes from the center outward, then spins a spiral around and around the spokes until the web is done. When an insect gets caught in the web, the spider often ties up the victim with more silk.

Spiderwebs are very fragile. The spider has to continually repair the web or spin a new one. A life built without Christ is like a spiderweb—fragile. But a life built on him is a life built on the Rock.

Think about what God says to you

Such is the fate of all who forget God. The hope of the godless comes to nothing. Everything they count on will collapse. They are leaning on a spiderweb.

Job 8:13-14

Do you sometimes rely on everything except God? Especially in a crisis, you might say to yourself: *I don't have* time *to rely on God and wait for his timing. I have to do something right now!* But that kind of thinking is like leaning on a spiderweb.

Let's talk to God!

MY JOURNAL (choose one)

I remember when I felt as if I didn't have time to talk to you, God, about what to do, and I made this decision without asking for your help:

_____

_____

_____

_____

_____

I remember a time when I asked you, God, to help me figure out what to do. This is what happened:

_____

_____

_____

_____

_____

MY PRAYER

Dear God, the life that's made apart from you is as fragile as a spider's web. The life that's built on you is as strong as a rock.

■ ■

Experiment: Web Crawling

Ever wonder why spiders don't get stuck in their own webs? Let's find out:

1. Ask your mom or dad if you can use some Scotch tape, a piece of dark-colored construction paper, and a little drop of cooking oil.
2. Take a piece of the Scotch tape about six inches long and stick it down in the middle of the paper. Then take a second piece the same length and stick it on too, making a plus sign.
3. Take two more pieces of tape and stick them on top of the plus sign to make an X. Your "web" should look like the spokes of a wheel.
4. Tap along the tape with your finger.
5. Take a fifth piece of tape and put it across the other pieces of tape, sticky side up, turning the two ends of the tape under so it sticks to the paper.
6. Tap on this piece of tape with your finger.
7. Now put your finger in that drop of cooking oil and tap your finger on the sticky tape again. What happens?

The spider spins its web with non-sticky strands that go out like the spokes of a wheel, and then fills in with sticky strands that go around the spokes, connecting them.

The spider knows to stay on the non-sticky strands. But even if it walks on the sticky strands, it probably won't get stuck because of a special oily substance it has on its feet!

COSMIC
Curiosities

**When they saw the star,
they were filled with joy!**

Matthew 2:10

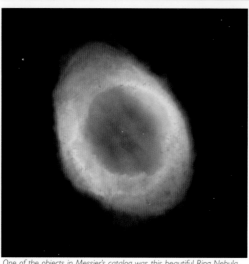

One of the objects in Messier's catalog was this beautiful Ring Nebula.
(HST photo courtesy Space Telescope Science Institute)

Charles Messier (MESS-ee-yay) was born in 1730 and grew up with eleven brothers and sisters in a home that was probably pretty messy. But that's not why he was named Messier; it was just the family name. Charles became interested in stars and planets because of a six-tailed comet that flew by Earth when he was fourteen. When he was twenty-one, he went to Paris and got a job at an observatory. He began to search for Halley's Comet in 1757. Many years before, Edmund Halley had predicted the comet would return in that year. Instead of finding the comet through his telescope, Messier discovered many glowing mystery blobs. To Messier, these objects looked like comets—dim, fuzzy things flying through space—but he discovered that they weren't. Messier was a comet hunter, though, and he wanted to help people who were looking for comets not to be fooled by these fuzzy blobs that were not comets. So he wrote about them all in a book. He made a great catalog of 103 objects.

As telescopes became bigger and better, people began to see that Messier's objects were actually strange and wonderful worlds. Some turned out to be galaxies—great pinwheels of stars far away. Others were nebulae—clouds of glowing gases. Still others were globular clusters—groups of hundreds of thousands of stars. To this day many of the objects which

Messier put in his catalog are known by the numbers he gave them. For example, M31 is the Andromeda Galaxy, and M1 is the Crab Nebula. All of the fuzzy blobs Messier saw have turned out to be beautiful, intricate jewels in the night sky.

Sometimes our view of God is a little bit fuzzy. Sometimes we're not sure just what we are looking at. But the Bible is like a strong telescope. When we look through it, we can begin to see God much more clearly. Look through your Bible "telescope" for a few minutes every day, and you'll be amazed at how God begins to come into focus.

Think about what God says to you

> Jesus replied, "You are in error because you do not know the Scriptures or the power of God."
> Matthew 22:29, NIV

Jesus said this to a group of Sadducees who were asking him questions. They did not believe in heaven because they were thinking in human terms. They had not read the Bible to learn what God has to say and to understand his power.

Let's talk to God!

MY JOURNAL (choose one)

This is one time I made up my own idea about you, God, instead of looking through the "telescope" of my Bible:

_____

_____

_____

_____

This is something I learned about you, God, when I looked through the "telescope" of my Bible:

_____

_____

_____

_____

_____

MY PRAYER

Lord, I want to spend more time with you, getting to know you through the pages of the Bible.

DAY 2: THE EAGLE NEBULA
LAYS STAR EGGS!

Stars are being born in the so-called "Pillars of Creation" in the Eagle Nebula. (See Week 13 opening photo.)

Naming nebulae requires the same active imagination that naming constellations does. For example, from a certain angle, the Eagle Nebula looks a little bit like an eagle, so that's what it's called. But the most interesting thing about this nebula isn't its name; it's the massive columns of gas rising up inside the nebula. They are called the Pillars of Creation, and with good reason. These magnificent columns are a nursery for hatching stars. Scientists call these new baby stars "evaporating gaseous globules"— EGGs for short!

The formation of these stars is a complex dance of death and life. We know that God formed everything in the universe out of two gases: hydrogen and helium. Some of the first stars were glowing Goliaths made up of these light gases. After a while, these big hydrogen and helium stars became unstable and exploded. Stars that explode are called *supernovae*. (Smaller stars die out in more quiet ways—see Day 3.) Here's the tricky part: As a star burns, its gases are forced together to make molecules of heavier elements that can come together to make metals and rocks. When a star explodes, these elements from the blown-apart star drift through space in great clouds called *nebulae*. As the molecules are attracted to each other, the clouds condense, eventually becoming stars like our sun. We know our sun is a star that formed from these heavier gases because our solar system has heavy elements like nickel and iron. The little starlets in the Eagle Nebula's Pillars of Creation will become stars too. They are made from the gases of dead stars that exploded and bonded together into heavier elements. Without the heavy elements in these gases, the new stars could not have heavy things like planets going around them. If our sun had not been born of materials from dead stars, our wonderful Earth with its solid surface and metallic core wouldn't be here. It's an amazing feature of God's cosmic design.

From the death of ancient stars came our own living planet, whirling around a life-giving sun. It's another reminder to us that with God, life can come from death. The most important example of this in our lives is the death and resurrection of God's Son, Jesus, who died and lived again so that we could live forever with him. Jesus' death on the cross was not the end, but just the beginning of the adventure for Christ-followers. From Jesus' death came eternal life for believers everywhere.

Think about what God says to you

And with [Christ] you were raised to a new life because you trusted the mighty power of God, who raised Christ from the dead.
Colossians 2:12

Our new life in Christ means that our old, sinful life is dead and buried. We can still choose to sin, but we don't have to. Christ is there to help us fight off the urge to sin and choose to live a new way.

Let's talk to God!

MY JOURNAL (choose one)

This is something in my life that I am ready to give up on. I know that you can "bring life," God, and change the situation so that I can have hope again:

_____

_____

_____

_____

This is a time when I gave up on something and thought it was "dead," but you made things right again, God:

_____

_____

_____

_____

MY PRAYER

God, I am not perfect. There are so many times when I choose the wrong way. The Bible says that "this way brings death." Thank you that Jesus has taken away my sins and that you will help me decide to do the right and good things in my life. Thank you for being a God who can make life out of death and hope out of hopelessness.

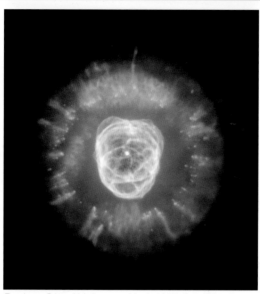

The elegant Eskimo Nebula, captured by the Hubble Space Telescope, is an expanding cloud of gas around a dying star. (HST photo courtesy of Space Telescope Science Institute.)

Until the Hubble Space Telescope was up and running, nobody guessed how strange the Eskimo Nebula really is. First spotted in 1787 by William Herschel, the same guy who discovered Uranus, the nebula got its nickname because it looks like a face surrounded by a parka's fur hood.

The Eskimo Nebula is called a planetary nebula because it's roundish like a planet. The parka of this Eskimo is a see-through globe of material that was blown away from the surface of a dying star about ten thousand years ago. That star is in the middle of the nebula, and its light makes the gases around it glow. The nebula is really shaped like an hourglass, with two gigantic bubbles of gas above and below the star. Each bubble is one light-year long! But the hourglass shape is pointed toward us so we can see only part of both megabubbles. Deep inside the cloud of gas, close to the star, are squiggly trails of hot star-stuff that look like balls of string. There are also mysterious, comet-shaped blobs in the parka. These may be fast-moving gas lumps that are running into slow-moving gases, which came from the star earlier. By studying the light from the nebula, scientists can tell that the Eskimo Nebula is five thousand light-years away. In other words, it would take five thousand years to travel from Earth to the nebula at the speed of light. The light we are seeing left the Eskimo Nebula five thousand years ago, when people were just starting to build temples in Babylon.

The star in the Eskimo Nebula is much older than our own sun. Learning about this cool cosmic customer teaches us what to expect when our own sun gets to that same age in five or six billion years. In the same way, God puts older people in your life so you can learn from them about the different seasons of life that you will be moving through as you get older.

Think about what God says to you

> *Remember the days of long ago; think about the generations past. Ask your father and he will inform you. Inquire of your elders, and they will tell you.*
> *Deuteronomy 32:7*

Think for a few minutes about the people you know. Are they all the same age? No way! God has given you a lot of people to know in a lot of different seasons of life. He did this for a reason—he wants you to be able to learn from them what to expect at each stage of your life, to help you get ready for those stages. How cool is that?

Let's talk to God!

MY JOURNAL (choose one)
Show me someone in high school who loves you, God. I want to ask about this part of what it's like to be in high school:

_____

_____

_____

_____

Help me, God, to think of someone in college who can tell me about this:

_____

_____

_____

_____

Lead me to a person who is single and works at an interesting job. This is something I really want to know about being young, single, and working:

_____

_____

_____

_____

I'd like you to put me in touch with a young married couple that loves you, God. This is something I want to learn from them about dating:

_____

_____

_____

_____

MY PRAYER

Dear God, thank you for putting older people in my life. I can learn a lot from them about what things will be like for me as I grow up. Please give me the courage to talk to them about questions I have.

The galaxy group known as Abell 2218 warps space around it. Distant galaxies look like arcs of light swirling around the galaxies at center left. (HST photo courtesy of Space Telescope Science Institute.)

In 1915 a really brainy guy named Einstein wrote the theory of relativity. His theory had nothing to do with uncles or mother-in-laws or other relatives. Instead, it described how time, matter, gravity, and light are all related.

One prediction of Einstein's theory was that if something had a lot of gravity, it would actually bend space around it. If he was right, light waves would curve around the dip in space made by a heavy object. Many years later, scientists were able to show that when stars go behind the sun (which has a *lot* of gravity), their positions seem to shift. This is because their light is being bent around the sun, so we can see around the sun's edge. Bent starlight around the sun proves that Einstein was right about gravity being able to bend light!

The warping of light around a heavy object in space is called *gravitational lensing.* Here is one way to think of it: Picture the bed of a trampoline as a plane of light waves. Then picture yourself standing on the trampoline. Gravity pulls you down into it, and the light waves

231

bend a little around your feet. Next, instead, picture your mom or dad standing on the trampoline. They are heavier than you are, so their gravitational pull is stronger and bends the light waves more.

Scientists have found an even more spectacular example of gravitational lensing farther out in space. When the Hubble Space Telescope turned its powerful gaze on a cluster of galaxies called Abell 2218 (such a nice name for a bunch of galaxies!), it found that more distant galaxies could be seen around it. The far galaxies look like glowing streaks warped around the Abell galaxy cluster. Thanks to the gravity of Abell 2218, the distant galaxies are magnified. Scientists have found over fifty of these remote, young galaxies through the cosmic zoom lens of Abell 2218.

Just as the gravitational lensing of the galaxies of Abell 2218 helps us to see what is beyond them, God has arranged things in life so that we can see him. We can't see gravitational lensing, but we can see its effect. And although we can't see God with our eyes, we can see the effects of his power. The famous poet Ralph Waldo Emerson said, "All I have seen teaches me to trust the Creator for all I have not seen."

Think about what God says to you

It was by faith that Moses left the land of Egypt.
He was not afraid of the king. Moses kept right on going
because he kept his eyes on the one who is invisible.
Hebrews 11:27

How could Moses keep his eyes on someone who is invisible? He could trust God to be with him because he had seen the proof of God's existence in the burning bush, in the miracle of the staff that became a snake, and in the miraculous plagues that fell on Egypt.

Let's talk to God!

MY JOURNAL (choose one)

Lord, I can tell you are working in this world when I see:

_____

_____

_____

_____

Here are some ways that you show yourself to me:

_____

_____

_____

_____

MY PRAYER

God, you show me your power in many ways—by healing sick people, by the changed lives of the people you save, by all the prophecies that Jesus fulfilled, and by keeping all your promises to me. Thank you.

A black hole at the center of the giant galaxy M87 can be seen as a bright spot. A powerful jet of glowing gas is shooting out of the center and up toward the right. This stream of material is thousands of light-years long. (HST photo courtesy of Space Telescope Science Institute.)

When you open a box full of chocolates, the first thing you want to do is find out what's in the middle of each piece. Does it have a chewy center? Are there nuts? Caramel? It's easy and fun to find out. All you have to do is bite in and taste! Scientists want to find out what's in the middle of the Milky Way—not the candy bar, but the place we call home. The Milky Way is a great spiral of stars called a galaxy. It's shaped like a disk with a bulge in the middle, and it stretches 90,000 light-years across. That's 529,020,000,000,000,000 (529,020 trillion) miles! Our sun, with Earth tagging along, floats around about halfway out from the center, 27,000 light-years from the mystery middle. But finding out what's in the middle of this Milky Way isn't as easy as a taste test. Between earth and the middle of the galaxy are many stars and streams of dark clouds like the Eagle Nebula (Day 2).

If we look up and out of our galaxy we can see the centers of other galaxies much farther away. What we find is strange, weird, and wonderful. Many large galaxies have cores that put out a lot of energy, as if millions of stars were pumping out radiation all at once. In many cases the energy is so fierce that it can't be explained away by normal stars. The Hubble Space Telescope has found evidence of a black hole in the massive galaxy M87. As we saw in *Absolutely Awesome I,* a black hole is a star so massive that it actually sucks light into it. A black hole also develops a disk of swirling material around it that throws off deadly radiation, and it is often this radiation that we "see." A disk of gas spirals around the center of M87 at 1.2 million miles per hour! The object at the center of M87 weighs as much as 3 billion suns concentrated into a neighborhood only the size of our little solar system.

Is there a black hole at the center of our galaxy? Many scientists say, "You betcha!" Infrared imagers on the Hubble Telescope can look through those dark clouds that hide the galaxy's center. Scientists have detected an oddball source of radiation pulsating at the Milky Way's core. They think the radiation comes from a disk of matter twirling around a black hole two and a half million times as dense as our sun.

At the core of each galaxy is a mysterious energy source that holds the galaxy together and keeps it from flying apart. As Christians, we too have a powerful central energy source.

Think about what God says to you:

I myself no longer live, but Christ lives in me.
So I live my life in this earthly body by trusting in the
Son of God, who loved me and gave himself for me.
Galatians 2:20

You are controlled by the Spirit if you have the Spirit of God
living in you. . . . Since Christ lives within you, even though
your body will die because of sin, your spirit is alive
because you have been made right with God.
Romans 8:9-10

God provides us with his power through his Son and his Holy Spirit living in us and controlling us. God's power can cheat death and conquer sin! With this power at our center, we never need to worry or panic.

Let's talk to God!

MY JOURNAL (choose one)

This is what your Word in Galatians 2:20 means to me:

_____

_____

_____

_____

This is what you say to me in Romans 8:9-10:

_____

_____

_____

_____

MY PRAYER

God, thank you for giving me your Son, Jesus. He wants to be the center of my life. All I need to do is ask him. I will never be alone with Jesus living in me. He gives me the power I need for living and the hope I need for the future.

Light-Years!

Distances in space are so great that we measure them by light-years. A light-year is the distance it takes light to travel in one year, which is about 5.878 trillion miles. The star nearest to us, Proxima Centauri, is 4.2 light-years away. As soon as you try measuring it with a yardstick, you'll see why astronomers decided to use light-years instead.

Experiment: Let's Bend Some Light!

By using a flashlight and a glass of water, you can show the way light is bent around heavy objects like black holes or galaxy clusters. We will not be bending light by using gravity, but rather by using water. This kind of light bending is different than what happens around a galaxy, but it is a good model for what happens out in space.

FOR THIS ACTIVITY YOU WILL NEED:
- a flashlight
- a table
- a comb
- a glass of water

1. Turn off all the lights in the room so that it is really dark. Turn on the flashlight and lay it flat on the table. You should see the flashlight beam spreading across the surface of the table.
2. Now hold a comb right against the front of the flashlight so that the light casts narrow beams across the table.
3. Put a glass of water about an inch in front of the comb and watch what happens to the light beams. They should bend toward each other. In our model, we use a flashlight and a glass of water to represent the far-away galaxy light and the galaxy cluster that bends the light. Which is the flashlight? The glass?

Note: You may want to review what you learned on Day 2 of Week 5 about light bending. The topic there was "Mirages—Vanishing Mirrors." Remember that galaxies and black holes bend light through gravity!

If you enjoyed ABSOLUTELY AWESOME 2,
check out these other great devotionals
for kids and families!

Absolutely Awesome
0-8423-3043-7

INDEX OF BIBLE VERSES

Week 7:Botany 101
VERSE FOR THE WEEK

Genesis 2:8-9

DAILY VERSES

Matthew 13:24-29

Philippians 4:7

Revelation 22:2

1 Corinthians 3:6

Daniel 1:18-20

Week 8:The Mammals
VERSE FOR THE WEEK

Psalm 36:6

DAILY VERSES

Proverbs 17:17

Ephesians 6:10-11

Isaiah 49:15

1 Corinthians 7:25

Galatians 5:1

Week 9:Deserts
VERSE FOR THE WEEK

Isaiah 43:19-20

DAILY VERSES

Matthew 6:19-21

Habakkuk 1:5

2 Peter 3:8

Jeremiah 23:24

Ezekiel 36:26-27

Week 10:Tinkering with God's Design
VERSE FOR THE WEEK

Ecclesiastes 8:17

DAILY VERSES

John 11:52

1 Corinthians 6:12

Matthew 10:29-31

Ephesians 2:10

Psalm 77:14

Week 11:For the Birds
VERSE FOR THE WEEK

Genesis 1:20

DAILY VERSES

Genesis 8:8-12

Genesis 8:6-7

Psalm 9:9

Isaiah 40:31

Proverbs 23:22, 26

Week 12:Creepy Crawlies
VERSE FOR THE WEEK

Malachi 3:11

DAILY VERSES

John 16:33

2 Corinthians 6:14-16

Luke 1:78-79

Luke 11:11-13

Job 8:13-14

Week 13:Cosmic Curiosities
VERSE FOR THE WEEK

Matthew 2:10

DAILY VERSES

Matthew 22:29

Colossians 2:12

Deuteronomy 32:7

Hebrews 11:27

Galatians 2:20; Romans 8:9-10

INDEX OF SCIENTIFIC TERMS

ABOUT THE AUTHORS

Michael and Caroline Carroll are the authors of the first book in this series, *Absolutely Awesome I*. They are both freelance writers who hang out in Littleton, Colorado, with their son, Andy, and daughter, Allie. Two of their favorite places to visit in this awesome world are Iceland and Hawaii.

Michael is a science journalist and space artist with a bachelor of fine arts degree from Colorado State University. Prior to freelancing he served as a staff artist for the Reuben Fleet Science Center for ten years.

Some of the books that Michael has written are *Spinning Worlds, Volcanoes and Earthquakes,* and *Dinosaurs* (Chariot Victor Publishing). Some of the magazines for which Michael has done articles and paintings include *Astronomy, Popular Science, Smithsonian, Time,* and *Weekly Reader.* He has also created book illustrations for works by Carl Sagan, Arthur C. Clarke, Gil Morris, and Steven Lawhead, among others.

Michael has lectured at various schools and at the Denver Museum of Natural History. He has also led discipleship and home study ministries. For several years he has been an elder at Deer Creek Community Church in Littleton, Colorado.

Through this devotional, Michael is excited about the opportunity to "showcase God's spectacular universe." In addition to writing the book with his wife, he created the paintings that appear at the beginning of each week and took the photos that are not otherwise identi-fied. The goal that he and Caroline had when they wrote this book was to combine "the things we learn from nature with the spiritual truths of the Bible."

Caroline, also a graduate of Colorado State University, has been an occupational therapist but now focuses on writing full-time, along with being a full-time mom. She also enjoys painting with watercolors.

Caroline and her husband both have a strong science background and a desire to "encourage believers and unbelievers alike to learn more about the nature and power of God through the medium of science." She and Michael field-tested the books in this series with their children and their children's friends, finding that the devotionals worked well at dinnertime and led to "spirited discussion about the subject of the day." Doing the activities with their kids' friends also gave the family an opportunity to talk with other kids about God.

Caroline has been active at Deer Creek Community Church in many different areas, serving as a Sunday school teacher, choir member, home study leader, women's Bible study coordinator, and women's ministry activity coordinator. She has also participated in many school support functions and hosted Moms in Touch prayer groups.